Talking Points for Shakespeare Plays

What do students think about Shakespeare? Classic, timeless and full of rich ideas; or difficult, impenetrable and completely uninteresting?

This book aims to help young people develop a real interest in Shakespeare, based on their understanding and engagement with the texts. A meaningful classroom discussion that enables every individual to contribute, and covers a range of viewpoints, can help students' understanding of Shakespeare's plays, consolidate their learning and increase their motivation.

This highly practical book enables teachers to organise, stimulate and support group discussions that will help students to relate to the characters, and develop their own ideas about the language and meaning. Drawing on four of the most commonly taught Shakespeare plays, the book provides a broad range of exciting tried and tested resources, taking the reader through key parts of the text, along with suggestions for further activities involving writing, drama and electronic media.

Features include:

- Scene by scene Talking Points for each play
- Thinking Together extension activities for group work
- Guidance on developing your own Talking Points
- Talking Points focusing on Shakespeare's language use.

Offering an accessible, thought-provoking and above all enjoyable way for students to engage with Shakespeare's plays, this book will be highly beneficial reading for English teachers and trainees.

Lyn Dawes is a teacher and education consultant, specialising in Science and Talk for Learning. She is the author of a series of books dealing with classroom talk, notably *Talking Points: Discussion Activities in the Primary Classroom* (Routledge, 2012).

Talking Points for Shakespeare Plays

Discussion activities for *Hamlet*, *A Midsummer Night's Dream*, *Romeo and Juliet* and *Richard III*

Lyn Dawes

Routledge
Taylor & Francis Group

LONDON AND NEW YORK

First published 2013
by Routledge
2 Park Square, Milton Park, Abingdon, Oxon OX14 4RN

Simultaneously published in the USA and Canada
by Routledge
711 Third Avenue, New York, NY 10017

Routledge is an imprint of the Taylor & Francis Group, an informa business

British Library Cataloguing in Publication Data
A catalogue record for this book is available from the British Library

Library of Congress Cataloging in Publication Data
Dawes, Lyn.
  Talking points for Shakespeare plays: discussion activities for Hamlet, a
  Midsummer Night's Dream, Romeo and Juliet and Richard III/Lyn Dawes.
  p. cm.
  Includes bibliographical references.
  1. Shakespeare, William, 1564–1616 – Study and teaching. 2. Discussion –
  Study and teaching – Activity programs. I. Title.
  PR2987.D39 2013
  822.3′3 – dc23
  2012039551

ISBN: 978-0-415-52542-8 (hbk)
ISBN: 978-0-415-52543-5 (pbk)
ISBN: 978-0-203-11983-9 (ebk)

Typeset in Bembo and Helvetica
by Florence Production Ltd, Stoodleigh, Devon, UK

Printed and bound in Great Britain by
TJ International Ltd, Padstow, Cornwall

For Claire

Contents

Contents

Contents

Introduction

EDUCATION AND SHAKESPEARE'S PLAYS

What distinguishes an educated person? The philosopher and poet Samuel Taylor Coleridge thought that it was not breadth of knowledge, or having in your mind a catalogue of information – but instead the capacity to order and relate facts and ideas, and to grasp the underlying principles that generate them. His 1812 lectures on *Hamlet* inspired great interest and provided a basis for a deeper understanding of both the characters and the essence of the play. Previously *Hamlet* had been heavily criticised and misunderstood. 'A monstrous farce, scattered with terrible soliloquies' (Voltaire, 1727); 'Of the feigned madness of Hamlet there appears no adequate cause' (Dr Johnson, 1765); Hamlet himself had been dismissed by Goethe (1796) as 'a weak man incapable of rising to the demands of historical destiny'; and his character was regarded as corrupt – 'Hamlet has a natural inclination to devious behaviour' (Schlegel, 1798) (all above citations in Holmes, 1998: 282–3).

But Coleridge reflected on the actual words that Shakespeare had written, and through the words, the characters he had created. Coleridge considered Hamlet's inward-looking soliloquies, his relationships with other characters and his mix of inaction and action to be the products of a great mind under extreme pressure.

> In *Hamlet* I conceive [Shakespeare] to have wished to exemplify the moral necessity of a due balance between our attention to outward objects and our meditation on inward thoughts – a due balance between the real and the imaginary world. In *Hamlet* this balance does not exist
>
> (Coleridge quoted in Holmes, 1998: 286).

Coleridge's perceptive reflections on *Hamlet* have informed attitudes towards the play ever since. In this book, I make practical use of his idea that the educated

1

mind is one that 'has been accustomed to contemplate not things only, or for their sake alone, but likewise and chiefly the relations of things' (Coleridge quoted in Holmes, 1998: 481). The Talking Points based on Shakespeare's *Hamlet* are intended to encourage students to examine the play's words and ideas, so that they can establish a deeper understanding of the drama that is happening in Hamlet's mind – and on the stage. Similarly, Talking Points for *Romeo and Juliet*, *A Midsummer Night's Dream* and *Richard III* provide stimulus so that students can share thoughts about the proceedings of the plays and the motivation and emotions of the characters. Sharing ideas aloud helps students to express tentative ideas and to compare and contrast what they are thinking with what they hear. The Talking Points create the need to use both the text and the imagination, to apply imagination to what individuals or the group know of the play. What students know will depend on their reading and their own lived experience. This creative mixing of imagination and reality provides the material for the real power of discussion. An equitable discussion can enable students to air their knowledge in a context that encourages questioning, challenge and synthesis of ideas. Students talking to one another are also developing new ways to think about a range of ideas. A good discussion is an educational experience, creating educated minds.

We want all students to have the opportunity to gain insight into Shakespeare's work. It is no good if only the bright, the privileged and the diligent do so without taking others along with them. Shakespeare can speak to all of us. There is no reason why every student should not have access to the experience of understanding *Hamlet*, or enjoying *A Midsummer Night's Dream*. We want to ensure that every student has the opportunity to delve into the plays with an interested group who share their ideas openly.

There is more to be gained during discussion than access to Shakespeare. A shared understanding of ourselves as characters and our lives as influenced by the times and context we find ourselves in can arise from talking about the people in the plays. Shakespeare's gift is to offer everyone a perspective on themselves and others, and an understanding of humanity based on acknowledging unity while accepting diversity. There is also the chance simply to gain knowledge. Coleridge thought that knowledge could never be 'infused or impressed' but that it might be 'trained, fed or excited' (1812). Talking with others provides individuals with the chance to train their minds to think, question and speculate, to elaborate, analyse and synthesise new ideas. Talking about Shakespeare stimulates an appetite for learning. Excitement comes from seeing the point of the words, a scene, a character, the entire play – or from seeing that there are straightforward ways to gain direct access to the ideas of others and to have an impact on others as you articulate your own ideas. In addition, the rich language and the way words are used in the plays provide a permanent mental resource for all who have heard and understood them. Talking to others, using and discussing Shakespeare's vocabulary and his way of turning a phrase or offering a metaphor, can help students to assimilate words and ideas for their own subsequent use.

With the Talking Points as stimulus and Shakespeare's words as a focus, a student can become educated in the most profound sense of the word. As the group reflects on their own ideas and those of others, individuals see that there are ways to develop what they understand. Discussion is a resource for later introspection. It also supports writing. By talking about the play, students gain insight into the impact of thought on action. They can usefully recognise that post-action rationalisations may take the place of considered forethought in ordinary lives. They can begin to question their own reasoning and logic in ways that give them chances to see others doing the same. Such exploratory discussions are an essential part of the education of young people. Education in this sense is transferable between contexts, applicable to any area of learning, and a development of the mind's powers to understand the real world and the abstract principles that influence thought and action.

Students using the Talking Points need ready access to Shakespeare's play texts. They also need to know what we mean when we ask them to discuss their ideas with a group.

PREPARING STUDENTS FOR 'A GOOD DISCUSSION'

What is 'a good discussion'? For students asked to work in talk groups, an awareness of what makes a good discussion is essential. Students may well be able to tell you what they think constitutes 'a good discussion' – but in practice it might be anything from difficult to impossible for them to generate or take part in such discussion. The problems they encounter may include, for example, social pressures and lack of confidence. One factor that makes the most difference to students trying to establish discussion is the knowledge that all members of their group share the same ideas about talk for learning. So, before discussion, it is worth checking if everyone agrees what makes a good discussion, and ensuring that all will aim for high quality, exploratory talk.

Exploratory talk is educationally effective talk. Everyone contributes and everyone listens attentively. The group stays on task. Each person is asked directly for their ideas. The group offers a chance to express tentative ideas; there is respect for what is said and individuals can change their minds when presented with an attractive or robust alternative. Learning arises from the chance to think aloud. Importantly, there is an expectation that reasons will be offered or asked for. A degree of challenge is both expected and valued – agreement is eventually sought, but only when all variations and alternatives have been carefully considered. Students need to be open-minded and aware that everyone will gain from sharing all relevant information. Personal knowledge is a resource for the group, not an end in itself. Students elaborate, chain ideas together and provide explanation. Each group member is expected to be able to summarise and communicate the gist of the group's discussion.

Listening and turn taking are key skills, along with the ability to link ideas together and to summarise points that others have made. In a talk group setting, every student should know that they are responsible for their own learning and that of others – quite a responsibility; but a very heady experience. Talk groups should tackle the Talking Points knowing that any one of them will be expected to contribute their ideas to a whole-class plenary discussion.

In summary, exploratory talk can help students to think and develop new ideas by taking other points of view into account. In exploratory talk:

- each group member understands the importance of discussion;
- everyone contributes;
- contributions are invited, and carefully attended to;
- all shared ideas are respected;
- reasons are offered for opinions;
- challenges are valued as a way of stimulating thinking;
- disagreement is worded to enable further discussion;
- ideas are linked through talk;
- contributors are given time to develop their ideas and elaborate on what they say;
- the group works together to negotiate a shared outcome.

Discussion based on exploratory talk enables *interthinking* – that is, shared thinking aloud. Interthinking provides individuals with opportunities to:

- articulate their own ideas, comparing them with others;
- analyse and evaluate a wider range of points of view;
- elaborate and explain in ways that establish cogent arguments;
- better understand the thinking of others;

- see ways to create a new, shared response by chaining or intertwining group ideas. (See Mercer and Littleton, 2007.)

When working with Talking Points, students will use direct evidence from the plays, bringing in information from personal study, and their understanding of other material such as theatre productions, film clips and critical texts to support their thinking and reasoning. Students should be aware that the learning aims of their group work are:

- to engage wholeheartedly with Shakespeare's writing;

- to prepare to share ideas in a whole-class discussion or forum;

- to establish a depth of understanding that will inform their work in drama;

- to share thinking so that the group can subsequently help with writing.

ABOUT THE TALKING POINTS

Talking Points are thought-provoking statements. Initially you might find it helpful to remind students of key phrases that will enable them to generate exploratory talk. Proficient use of such phrases – or 'talk tools' – is a life skill. (See Dawes, 2012.)

Useful talk tools include:

'What do you think? Why do you think that?'

'I agree with this, because . . .'

'I disagree with this, because . . .'

'This reminds me . . .'

'Can you say more about . . .'

'Can you explain . . .'

'What does anyone think of that idea?'

'I know that . . .'

'I am not sure about . . .'

'I have no idea and need to find out about . . .'

'Do we all think . . . ?'

During discussion time, the talk group *should not write anything down.*

Writing influences thinking; the writer may become a scribe, and not contribute ideas; the discussion may be halted while ideas are written; the writer may record their own thoughts rather than what they hear. Noting ideas is of course useful on many occasions, but in exploratory discussion writing only impedes the creation, exchange and synthesis of ideas. Shared memory of the conversation will help groups to record key points of the discussion later, if necessary.

Responding to Talking Points sometimes involves considering if the statement is 'right' or 'wrong', or if the group is 'uncertain'. Students should be aware that expressing uncertainty is helpful because it creates the conditions for further research, thinking and learning.

Talking Points lists are always rather long, because it is important that all groups have interesting ideas to consider and discuss for the time available. Until students learn how to conduct an exploratory discussion, they may tend to close down discussion by for example coming to a superficial agreement, or not asking one another to contribute. Having plenty to talk about means that that there is time for the teacher to support struggling groups in their exploratory talk, re-starting their thinking, offering key talk phrases, and asking them to consider ideas more deeply.

A group of three students is ideal. Fours tend to separate into two pairs, and more than four means that not all ideas will be heard. Pairs can conduct exploratory talk but the addition of a third person often provides stimulus, creative friction, and a breadth of experience, to enrich the discussion. The physical space available and a professional knowledge of how students respond to one another will inform practical decisions about the constitution of the talk groups.

Timing is crucial. It is of course impossible to predict how long any discussion might last. Fortunately teachers have a professional knowledge of their class coupled with an instinct for what is an optimal time for classroom based activities. In general, the group discussion of Talking Points may be 15–30 minutes, with the whole class plenary discussion a similar length of time.

ABOUT THINKING TOGETHER

Thinking Together activities are *extension* suggestions for group work, which may involve drawing or noting ideas.

INTRODUCING TALKING POINTS TO YOUR STUDENTS

1   Establish talk groups of students. Talk with the class about the impact talk has on learning. Mention or give examples of talk tools. Ask groups to talk together to generate a joint response to these ideas then share ideas with the whole class:

Talking Points: about talk

- It is easy to find out what other people think and know.
- It is better to keep your thoughts to yourself rather than sharing ideas.
- It is rude to disagree with someone else's ideas.
- Some people are naturally good at talking; others will never learn.
- Everyone has an opinion.
- We learn by reading, not by talking.
- We can say what makes a good discussion.

2   Ask your class to generate a set of five or six 'rules' for group discussion.

3   Conduct an exploratory discussion with the whole class, as a model for group work. Show groups a set of Talking Points related to the text you are studying. Work with them as a whole class to discuss the ideas, explicitly using talk skills to ask for ideas, ask for clarification and reasons, include everyone, link several ideas, and decide on a joint response.

4   Make sure that students know that they are expected to stay on task, and that any one of them may be asked to contribute to a whole class feedback session.

5   Share the 'Student Instructions' with the groups.

Ask talk groups to discuss a set of Talking Points. Ask a student to start by reading one point out loud and asking, 'What do you think?'

Try to visit groups as they talk, to get a flavour of each group's discussion, making a mental note of key points to raise in the plenary session.

6   Ask groups who are finding discussion difficult to refer to the class rules, or to spend some time acting as observers in functional groups so that they learn how to take part.

7   Close the group discussions and move into whole-class discussion based on one Talking Point. Ask for contributions from each group and summarise what you hear. Orchestrate further discussion using your notes from the group work session. Discuss more of the Talking Points if there is time.

8   Ask for students' ideas about what they have learned about the play. Also ask for examples of effective talk e.g. a good question, a clear idea, something well explained, a good summary, a good listener or what individuals have heard or learned from one another. Establish and reinforce the idea that exploratory talk enables learning. Remind students that they will be learning about *Hamlet*, or about how to have an educationally effective discussion – or both.

STUDENT INSTRUCTIONS FOR TALKING POINTS DISCUSSIONS

How to get the most from Talking Points

➤ With your group, discuss the Talking Points using exploratory talk.

➤ Remember that your contribution will help others to learn.

➤ Use your memory; nothing will be written down till later.

➤ Any one of you may be asked to contribute to the plenary discussion.

- First choose a reader and read and listen to the Talking Point.
- Now think about what this means in relation to the play text.
- Think how you can put your knowledge or opinions into words.
- Give reasons for what you say.
- Ask questions.
- Concentrate.
- Reflect on what you hear.
- Share what you think with your group.
- Listen attentively to others and match or contrast what they say with your own thoughts.
- Ask one another to explain, say more, or clarify what has been said.
- Sum up the discussion.
- Try to establish an agreement.
- Decide what you will say in the whole class discussion.

WRITING YOUR OWN TALKING POINTS

1   Talking Points put students in the position of having to justify their ideas and articulate their thinking. Some texts merit discussion more than others; decide on a suitable scene, quotation or section of text that you will be teaching.

2   Use the text to help you to generate about ten *STATEMENTS* that will get students talking. It helps to think of the statements as having an answer 'true, false or unsure' – that is, as statements that can be rationally considered. If you find that it's easier to write questions, do so – then turn them into statements.

   Talking Points can be found by looking at commentary on the play, or reviews of staged versions of the play. The many statements made about Shakespeare's work are there to be discussed rather than taken as read.

   Talking Points can be created by using what students write or say. Their responses turned into statements ('Juliet is pathetic'; 'Hamlet is boring'; 'Oberon is sexist') can provide an opening for valuable discussion in which opinions must be justified.

3   Express your Talking Points simply and concisely. The language used should be straightforward, so that the students have a way in to engaging with the complex ideas you want them to think about.

4   Think of an extension Thinking Together activity. This will involve the group using their ideas to create something or do further work together. This is so that those who rush their discussion (a stage on the way to learning how to think aloud with others) are productively occupied while others talk.

5   Number the list of Talking Points for later reference in discussion.

Teaching students to create Talking Points

Creating questions and answers stimulates higher order thinking – that is, reflection, analysis and evaluation. To generate and phrase a question, a student must identify uncertainty. It is useful to consider what it is that you *don't* know and to put it in to words. Questions can be starters for Talking Points. The nature of a *question* is such that there is an implication of an *answer*. Questions are not Talking Points.

It's a powerful thing for students to generate discussion points for their class. A structure based initially on questioning can help students to establish ideas that are worth discussing as Talking Points.

Getting started

Choose a section of text. Ask students to talk together in their groups to write five questions that they would like to ask other groups, each on a separate post-it note. These can be genuine questions, or things that the group can already answer.

Now ask the class to stick each of their post-its at the top of a sheet of A4 paper. Pass these around and ask students to discuss, reflect on and answer questions from other groups. Ensure that students are aware that the papers will ultimately be collected in as a resource.

Return the papers to their original groups.

Ask each group to talk about one of their questions and the sorts of answers that their classmates have offered. Ask what they have learned and who has helped them to learn. Bring out points about the ways questions are phrased, the difference between open and closed questions and the importance of questioning own knowledge to check for understanding and accuracy. Highlight uncertainty or 'don't know' answers as useful because they indicate important areas for future learning.

Generating Talking Points

Collect up the papers with questions and their answers. Using these as a resource, re-phrase as Talking Points for use in your next session. Students can do this task if you show them how.

Talking Points: *Hamlet*

Hamlet Talking Points scene by scene

HAMLET TALKING POINTS: ACT 1 SCENE 1

1 Horatio, Marcellus and Barnardo trust one another.

2 Marcellus and Barnardo expect Horatio to know what to do about the Ghost.

3 Horatio believes that they have seen a ghost.

4 Horatio's father was responsible for the war with Norway because he killed Fortinbras.

5 Horatio makes some sensible suggestions about what the Ghost might want to say.

6 It was unfriendly and reckless to decide to tell Hamlet that they had seen a ghost of his father; they could have waited for the next night to speak to it.

7 They are loyal, brave soldiers.

HAMLET TALKING POINTS: ACT 1 SCENE 2

1 Claudius felt that it was his duty to marry his dead brother's widow.

2 Claudius is afraid of war with Norway, so makes efforts to get out of it.

3 Laertes is a bit of a creep and 'sucks up to' Claudius.

4 Claudius and Gertrude are both annoyed by Hamlet's unhappiness.

5 A first impression of Hamlet is that he is rude and bad tempered.

6 Gertrude thinks Hamlet's behaviour is 'putting it on'.

7 Hamlet tries to tell his mother how he feels, but fails.

8 When Hamlet says he will obey his mother, he is being insolent.

9 Hamlet has no real friends, or he wouldn't talk to himself.

10 Hamlet is more upset about his mother's rapid marriage to his uncle, than he is about the death of his father.

11 Hamlet hates Claudius.

12 Hamlet does not believe that Horatio has seen the ghost of his father.

13 Hamlet was suspicious about the death of his father even before he saw Horatio.

THINKING TOGETHER: ACT 1 SCENES 1 AND 2

1 Draw a cartoon of the battlements; add characters with speech and thought bubbles. Discuss what each character says and thinks.

2 Draw a picture of the Ghost/King. Annotate with phrases from the text to show how the image of the Ghost is built up; and by using the description provided by Horatio.

HAMLET TALKING POINTS: ACT 1 SCENE 3

1   Laertes is bossy and hard hearted. He is under his father's thumb.

2   Laertes thinks Ophelia should do as he says. She is younger and weaker than he is, and so is the only person he can control.

3   Polonius gives Laertes good advice.

4   Laertes doesn't listen to a word Polonius says.

5   Polonius is even bossier than Laertes; he bullies Ophelia.

6   Ophelia likes Hamlet and is surprised by what her brother and father think.

7   Ophelia is pathetic.

THINKING TOGETHER: ACT 1 SCENE 3

1   Draw a cartoon of Polonius. In speech bubbles, create a set of instructions for Laertes in France – maybe starting with 'You must–' and 'You must not–'.

2   Think of three reasons why your group would like to have Laertes as their brother, and three reasons why you would not.

3   Imagine that Laertes is now in France. He wants to remind Ophelia not to trust Hamlet. Ophelia wants to remind him that he should take his own advice. Make up an exchange of text or email messages between the two of them.

HAMLET TALKING POINTS: ACT 1 SCENE 4

1 Hamlet gives good reasons for not liking the custom of celebrating by getting very drunk.

2 Hamlet is at first horrified by the Ghost, but because it looks like his father, puts aside his fear and insists on questioning it.

3 Hamlet is not really brave – he just does not value his own life.

4 Hamlet is filled with a sense of dread; he must take responsibility for vengeance in a way that is alien to his character.

5 The soldiers are wrong to disobey Hamlet's order to leave him ('I say, away!').

THINKING TOGETHER: ACT 1 SCENE 4

Draw a cartoon of Hamlet. Hamlet resists five attempts to stop him following the Ghost. Create five speech bubbles with words used to try to stop him. Think of another reason and add it. Also add what you think Hamlet says to justify following the Ghost.

HAMLET TALKING POINTS: ACT 1 SCENE 5

1 Hamlet already suspected Claudius of his father's murder.

2 The Ghost wants revenge on both Claudius and Gertrude.

3 The Ghost is more concerned about Claudius having stolen the kingship, than he is about Claudius marrying Gertrude.

4 The Ghost's story gives Hamlet purpose, courage and determination.

5 Hearing that his father was murdered, Hamlet is frantic and stupidly rejects the help of his friends.

6 Hamlet has no control over his speech and actions while he is so upset.

7 Horatio and the soldiers are baffled by the change in Hamlet.

THINKING TOGETHER: ACT 1 SCENE 5

1 Record King Hamlet's speech using sound and light effects.

2 Draw a cartoon of the scenes in the orchard.

HAMLET TALKING POINTS: ACT 2 SCENE 1

1 Polonius is being kind in sending Reynaldo to visit Laertes.

2 Polonius does not really like Laertes.

3 Ophelia should not tell her father about her friendship with Hamlet.

4 Ophelia self-centredly assumes that Hamlet's disturbed behaviour is to do with the way she has treated him.

5 Polonius is delighted to have something bad about Hamlet to report to Claudius.

THINKING TOGETHER: ACT 2 SCENE 1

Make a poster that advertises all the things Laertes could do during his trip to Paris.

HAMLET TALKING POINTS: ACT 2 SCENE 2

1 Rosencrantz and Guildenstern, childhood friends, are asked to spy on Hamlet.

2 Gertrude knows exactly why Hamlet is so upset.

3 Polonius reads out a private letter from Hamlet to Ophelia; Gertrude should have stopped this happening.

4 Both the King and the Queen find Polonius irritating.

5 Polonius is proud of having ended Ophelia's open friendship with Hamlet.

6 Even when acting mad, Hamlet gets the better of Polonius.

7 Polonius is unsure whether Hamlet is acting, or really mad.

8 Hamlet trusts Rosencrantz and Guildenstern.

9 Hamlet shows that he is not really mad by his intelligent interest in the travelling Players; he also makes it quite clear by his descriptions of himself.

10 Hamlet is thinking fast: while talking with the Players, he sees a way to confront Claudius and immediately acts on it.

11 Hamlet despises Polonius but tries to conceal it.

12 Hamlet, left alone, despairs and berates himself for his lack of action so far. He has the strength to make a plan involving the Players and is a little heartened by this.

13 Hamlet is sure that Claudius killed his father, the King.

HAMLET TALKING POINTS: ACT 3 SCENE 1

1 Claudius thinks Hamlet is pretending to be mad, and he's invited Rosencrantz and Guildenstern to act as spies.

2 Ophelia is enjoying being important and happily takes part in her father's plans.

3 Ophelia is deceitful and disloyal.

4 Hamlet knows that they are being watched. He is bitterly disappointed to find that Ophelia is untrustworthy.

5 Ophelia happily hands back the gifts Hamlet gave her.

6 Ophelia is sorry for herself after Hamlet has spoken to her.

7 Claudius makes a plan to send Hamlet overseas because he is, suddenly, afraid of him.

THINKING TOGETHER: ACT 3 SCENE 1

1 Draw a cartoon of Hamlet; annotate with thought bubbles containing his reasons why or why not to commit suicide, his ideas about life and death.

2 Ophelia writes a letter to the problem page of a teen magazine. Write the letter and the reply from an 'agony aunt' and responses from a range of readers.

HAMLET TALKING POINTS: ACT 3 SCENE 2

1 The play matters to Hamlet; he gives the actors clear instructions how to act.

2 Horatio is the only person Hamlet trusts.

3 Hamlet has already confided in Horatio about what the Ghost said. Neither of them is sure whether it was an 'honest' ghost, or telling lies; or imaginary.

4 Hamlet treats King Polonius, his mother and Ophelia equally rudely.

5 Hamlet is enjoying himself.

6 Hamlet's name for the play, '*The Mousetrap*' reveals his attitude to Claudius and his intention in helping to write the play.

7 Horatio understands the title of the play.

8 Hamlet wrote the Player Queen's lines that he interrupts by saying, 'That's wormwood, wormwood.'

9 The King and Queen are both startled by the content of the play and take it personally.

10 Hamlet is so excited by the success of his plot that he imagines he is in the play – he speaks in rhyme.

11 Hamlet should confront Claudius with his suspicions at this moment; it is impossible to understand why he does not.

12 Rosencrantz and Guildenstern, as Hamlet's childhood friends, are hurt by his distrust of them and this makes them more likely to spy on him for the King.

13 The comparison between playing an instrument and trying to make Hamlet snap out of his grief is enough to make Guildenstern ashamed.

14 Hamlet cares deeply for his mother and is trying to protect her.

THINKING TOGETHER: ACT 3 SCENE 2

1 From 'Speak the speech . . .' decide if you
think Hamlet has offered good advice to the
Players; what would you add or change?

2 Imagine that Guildenstern had been a really
skilled musician, able to play the pipe
Hamlet offers him. What would Hamlet have
said then?

3 If Hamlet had confronted Claudius at the
moment the King stopped the play, what
would he have said? What would Gertrude,
Polonius, Horatio and Ophelia say?
Create a three-minute play and act it out.

1 Hamlet turns out to have been right not to trust his former friends Rosencrantz and Guildenstern.

2 The King is aware that Hamlet has discovered his guilt.

3 Claudius does not regret what he has done; if he can get away with it, he will be perfectly happy.

4 Hamlet has been taught to believe that those who are at peace with God will go to heaven, and be there forever. This religious belief prevents him killing the King.

5 Hamlet is not worried about the idea that murdering Claudius would itself be a crime.

6 Claudius was not praying, just kneeling down with his thoughts elsewhere, so Hamlet should have killed him.

7 Polonius is interfering and silly, but not wicked.

THINKING TOGETHER: ACT 3 SCENE 3

1   Draw a cartoon of the King. Create thought
    bubbles; what has Claudius gained by his
    actions? What has he lost? What are his
    worries? What pleases him? What, on
    balance, does Claudius think of himself and
    his present state?

2   Create a Mind Map using these characters:
    Hamlet, Horatio, Ophelia, Laertes, Polonius,
    Gertrude, Claudius, Rosencrantz and
    Guildenstern, Soldiers, Players, Ghost.

    ■   Draw linking lines with a sentence
        saying how each relates to others.

    ■   Think of three describing words for each
        character.

    ■   Write a speech bubble for each
        character in which they explain
        themselves as if to a friend.

    ■   Choose a colour and signature tune for
        each person and say why.

3   Gertrude emails a Helpline about what she
    sees as her problem with Hamlet. Write the
    letter and the Helpline reply, with comments
    from other users of the Helpline site.

HAMLET TALKING POINTS: ACT 3 SCENE 4

1 By trusting Polonius, Gertrude shows that she is a very bad judge of character.

2 Gertrude is right to be afraid of Hamlet.

3 Hamlet knows it is Polonius behind the arras.

4 Hamlet has every right to be cruel to his mother; her quick re-marriage is a wicked thing even if she did not know that Claudius killed her husband.

5 Hamlet should talk straight; that would get Gertrude on his side.

6 The Ghost appears because Hamlet shows he cares more about Gertrude's hasty marriage than he does about the murder of his father.

7 Gertrude cannot see the Ghost because she is too wicked – only good people can see spirits.

8 Gertrude understands what Hamlet means about the contrast between her two husbands, even though she cannot see the Ghost.

9 Hamlet is pleased to be going to England with Rosencrantz and Guildenstern; he trusts them.

10 Hamlet insists that Gertrude should not tell Claudius about what he has told her.

11 Hamlet is sorry he has killed Polonius.

HAMLET TALKING POINTS: ACT 4 SCENE 1

1 Gertrude genuinely thinks that Hamlet is mad.

2 Claudius cares nothing for Polonius; he thinks only of his own safety and reputation.

HAMLET TALKING POINTS: ACT 4 SCENE 2

1 Hamlet despises Rosencrantz and ridicules him.

2 He has a clear idea of the true position of his former friends at court.

3 His clever insults show that he is far from mad.

4 Hamlet should not have left Denmark at this time.

HAMLET TALKING POINTS: ACT 4 SCENE 3

1 Hamlet hates Claudius and will not pay him the respect of speaking sensibly to him.

2 Hamlet does not mean it when he says, 'Good'.

3 Claudius has arranged Hamlet's death because he knows that Hamlet is likely to discover and reveal the murder he has already committed.

4 Claudius is very clever.

HAMLET TALKING POINTS: ACT 4 SCENE 4

1 Talking to the Captain, Hamlet shows that he is perfectly capable of reasoned conversation.

2 Hamlet believes that people are distinct from animals because they can think, which is right.

3 Hamlet believes himself to have shown cowardice - but he has not.

4 Hamlet has no plan at all about what to do next.

5 Hamlet thinks that the bitter dispute over some worthless land is a huge contrast with the way he has put off taking revenge for the crimes committed against him.

6 Hamlet admires the soldiers and their leaders, and approves of what they are doing.

HAMLET TALKING POINTS: ACT 4 SCENE 5

1 Gertrude does not want to see Ophelia because, after her talk with Hamlet, she is ashamed of herself.

2 Gertrude thinks Ophelia is insignificant and boring.

3 Ophelia's words and songs make no sense – but as the Gentleman points out, some sense can be gained from them.

4 The way Ophelia speaks here is very different from the way Hamlet talks when he appears 'mad'.

5 Gertrude thinks that Ophelia's insanity is a temporary effect.

6 Claudius manages to blame Hamlet for everything.

7 When Laertes bursts in, Gertrude grabs him, showing how much she cares for Claudius.

8 Laertes is furious; his response is very different from Hamlet's response to finding out about his father's death.

9 Laertes says he wants revenge no matter what the consequences.

10 Laertes is all talk.

11 Laertes thinks that Ophelia cannot face the horrors of reality.

12 Laertes makes no move to comfort Ophelia.

THINKING TOGETHER: ACT 4 SCENE 5

Make up the 'missing' scene between Laertes and Claudius to show how Claudius explains the death of Polonius.

HAMLET TALKING POINTS: ACT 4 SCENE 6

1 Hamlet can trust Horatio.

2 Hamlet's brief description of his voyage shows us that he is brave, quick-witted and admirable.

3 Hamlet has a clear idea of what he will do next.

THINKING TOGETHER: ACT 4 SCENE 6

Dramatise Hamlet's letter to Horatio.

HAMLET TALKING POINTS: ACT 4 SCENE 7

1 Claudius is being honest when he explains why he did not immediately punish Hamlet for killing Polonius.

2 Claudius confidently expects Laertes to hear that Hamlet has been killed at sea.

3 Claudius is horrified to hear that Hamlet has returned, and panics a bit.

4 Claudius immediately sees how he can put Laertes to use – to kill Hamlet.

5 Laertes is an expert with his sword, but is so used to being told what to do that he can easily be persuaded to mis-use this talent.

6 Laertes suggests poison on the tip of his sword; he has been corrupted by Claudius.

7 Claudius does not trust Laertes because he expects people to be as devious as himself.

8 The idea of giving Hamlet a poisoned drink shows that Claudius is getting reckless.

9 Gertrude tells of Ophelia's death first very bluntly, then in detail, which makes it seem almost like a pleasant journey.

10 Ophelia did not commit suicide.

11 Laertes is so full of the plan to kill Hamlet that he does not really care about the loss of Ophelia.

12 The idea that you can defer grief is ridiculous.

THINKING TOGETHER: ACT 4 SCENE 7

1   Illustrate (by writing, drawing or acting)
    these events:

    ■   Claudius reads Hamlet's letter.

    ■   Claudius and Laertes plan to kill Hamlet.

    ■   Ophelia drowns.

    Annotate your drawings by adding the
    thoughts of the characters you have
    drawn.

2   Think about Laertes and Ophelia. Create an
    alternative scene where Laertes reflects
    aloud on her death, asks questions of her
    maids, and says what he thinks about his
    sister, to show how he is really affected by
    her suicide.

HAMLET TALKING POINTS: ACT 5 SCENE 1

1 The First Clown is the Gravedigger; the Second Clown is his drinking mate.

2 The Gravedigger has no respect for Ophelia, or women in general.

3 The men resent the burial because they believe that a working-class woman would be treated differently.

4 Hamlet is appalled by the Gravedigger's indifference to the remains of the dead.

5 Hamlet believes that a person's character is represented by their skull, which should be handled with reverence.

6 Hamlet is at ease talking to the Gravedigger.

7 The Gravedigger is insolent.

8 Hamlet is amused by the idea that madness would go unnoticed in England.

9 Yorick's skull answers the puzzle Hamlet has already faced about what really happens to us after death.

10 Ophelia's funeral is a subdued and hasty affair because of how she died.

11 Hamlet is surprised to see Laertes and horrified to find that it is Ophelia's funeral.

12 To jump into a grave is a truly shocking thing to do, yet both Laertes and Hamlet do it.

13 Hamlet is now almost mad with grief, in a way he has not been before.

14 Hamlet loved Ophelia.

15 Hamlet cannot understand why Laertes is angry; he has forgotten about Polonius.

16 Hamlet fluently uses different kinds of talk when in conversation with people from different backgrounds in society.

17 Gertrude just doesn't understand Hamlet.

18 Gertrude is beginning to give up on Hamlet.

19 Claudius controls Laertes by reminding him of their murder plot.

THINKING TOGETHER: ACT 5 SCENE 1

1   Imagine how you might stage this very
    dramatic scene. Think together to come up
    with detailed stage directions.

2   Make up a conversation between the
    director of the play, using your stage
    directions, and the actor playing Hamlet, to
    support the actor in working out his feelings
    and how he will convey them.

3   Horatio says very little but, as Hamlet's
    only real friend, is very important. What is
    he thinking? Draw the scene with thought
    bubbles to show reflections and his ideas
    – his internal comments on the other
    characters, and on what is happening.

HAMLET TALKING POINTS: ACT 5 SCENE 2

1 Hamlet and Horatio believe that although people make their own choices about what to do and say, there is also a force that controls what goes on in our lives.

2 Life is full of chance events that nothing can control.

3 Hamlet's desire for revenge is stronger once he finds that Claudius gave orders to have him executed.

4 Rosencrantz and Guildenstern did not know what was in the letter.

5 Horatio questions whether Hamlet should have sent Rosencrantz and Guildenstern to their deaths.

6 Rosencrantz and Guildenstern deserve to die because they betrayed Hamlet.

7 Hamlet has no real respect for life, so death seems unimportant.

8 Hamlet's wish to restore his friendship with Laertes shows him to be sensitive, thoughtful and capable of admitting his own mistakes.

9 Claudius cleverly bets on Hamlet beating Laertes in a sword fight.

10 Horatio has a feeling that the idea of the sword fight is a trick.

11 Hamlet knows he is a better fencer than Laertes.

12 Hamlet wants to get things over with; he forsees his own death with equanimity.

13 Hamlet's apology to Laertes is genuine and generous.

14 Hamlet loyally tries to make amends to please Gertrude.

15 Laertes regrets his part in the murder plot, even before the fight begins.

16 Laertes is a cheat.

17 Hamlet refuses wine to indicate he will take nothing from Claudius.

18 Claudius kills Gertrude; he cares more for his kingship than for her.

19 No one really cares when Gertrude dies.

20 Gertrude alerts Hamlet to the murder plot; without her words, Claudius might have got away with it.

21 Laertes tries to make amends by telling Hamlet of the murder plot.

22 Hamlet, furious, finally takes revenge.

23 Laertes and Hamlet are reconciled.

24 Hamlet thinks dying is a good alternative to the torment of his life.

25 Horatio, heartbroken, cannot imagine life after the tragedy of losing Hamlet.

26 Hamlet's death is truly a tragedy.

27 Horatio accepts the responsibility to reveal the truth.

THINKING TOGETHER: ACT 5 SCENE 2

1 Horatio says that he can tell a story of these categories of death and incident: carnal, bloody and unnatural acts; accidental judgements, casual slaughters.

Think together about the following characters and events in the play, and decide which of Horatio's categories he will fit them into in the account he has promised Hamlet that he will give:

King Hamlet's death ■ the stabbing of Polonius ■ the appearance of the Ghost ■ Gertrude's wedding to Claudius ■ Ophelia's descent into insanity ■ Ophelia's drowning ■ Gertrude's death by poisoning ■ the letter with orders to murder Hamlet ■ the killing of Laertes ■ the use of Rosencrantz and Guildenstern to escort Hamlet ■ their death ■ the death of Hamlet.

2 Decide how Horatio might describe the death of Claudius to Fortinbras; act this or produce a storyboard.

3 Rewrite the last line of the play. Think of a fitting ending to the play that relates to the start of the play but does not involve firing guns.

More Thinking Together for *Hamlet*

1 TALKING POINTS: THOUGHTS ABOUT HAMLET

1 It is not surprising that Hamlet finds the idea of committing murder difficult – most people would.

2 Hamlet is a thoughtful, caring person.

3 Hamlet has had no help to get over his grief at the death of his father.

4 Gertrude has made the death of King Hamlet even more unbearable for Hamlet.

5 Hamlet's mother adores him.

6 His meeting with the Ghost gives Hamlet the right to be rude to his mother.

7 Hamlet is more interested in himself than in other people.

8 We see the best side of Hamlet when he is with Horatio.

9 Hamlet thinks Polonius is a fool and would never have wanted to have him as a father-in-law.

10 Hamlet's ideas about life and death change as a direct consequence of experience.

2 DEATH

Using Shakespeare's words, talk together to decide what Hamlet thinks about death, and what happens after death. Think about these scenes:

1 As we meet Hamlet (1,2).

2 When he kills Polonius (3,4).

3 Just before the play (3,1).

4 When he encounters Claudius praying (3,3).

5 When he meets the Gravedigger (5,1).

6 Just before his sword fight with Laertes (5,2).

7 After he has been poisoned (5,2).

3 COWARDICE

Hamlet asks, 'Am I a coward?' (2,2). He believes that thoughtful people can act in cowardly ways: 'Thus conscience does make cowards of us all' (3,1). He can see that what he understands as his cowardice may be to do with how he thinks.

> Now, whether it be
> Bestial oblivion, or some craven scruple
> Of thinking too precisely on the event,
> A thought which, quarter'd, hath but one part wisdom
> And ever three parts coward . . . (4,4)

- Think together to decide on a good working definition of 'coward' or 'cowardice'.

- Decide how well Hamlet fits your definition.

- Use the play text to find evidence for and against Hamlet's worry that he is a coward.

4 THOUGHTS ABOUT OPHELIA

Before Ophelia becomes mentally disturbed, she:

- takes Laertes' advice to be wary of Hamlet, and then accepts Polonius' ban on talking to him at all (1,3);

- is frightened by Hamlet looking at her intensely, despite the fact that she has rejected him (2,1);

- freely gives Polonius a letter in which Hamlet makes it clear that he loves her – 'I love thee best, O most best, believe it.' (2,2);

- conspires with Claudius, Polonius and Gertrude to deceive Hamlet into thinking he is alone with her (3,1);

- lies to Hamlet (3,1); and

- attempts to flirt with Hamlet during the play (3,2).

Decide what your group thinks of Ophelia by discussing these Talking Points.

Talking Points: Ophelia

1 We can say what sort of girl Ophelia is.

2 Ophelia was flattered by Hamlet's attention but did not fall in love with him.

3 It would be unfair to expect her to go against the advice of her brother.

4 Ophelia could not refuse to do as her father instructed.

5 She became part of a plot against Hamlet, but her motives were good.

6 She is a very silly person.

7 Ophelia had no friends.

8 Gertrude did not like Ophelia.

9 Ophelia is pure and innocent, and having to cope with real life unbalances her.

10 Ophelia's death was very beautiful.

11 Ophelia would have liked what happened at her funeral.

5 TALKING POINTS: HAMLET'S RELATIONSHIP WITH OPHELIA

When the play begins, Hamlet and Ophelia have exchanged tokens of love, despite knowing that they are not of the same social status. Their relationship then becomes one casualty of a series of horrific events.

Hamlet talks about their relationship:

> *I could interpret between you and your love, if I could see the puppets dallying. (3.2, 231)*

That is, he could make up a lover's dialogue between the two of them, if she wishes to carry on pretending to be in love. As the play scene goes on, and Hamlet is outrageously rude to her, Ophelia realises that he knows of her betrayal; and that their love is over.

Discuss the Talking Points to share your ideas about Hamlet and Ophelia's relationship.

Talking Points: Hamlet and Ophelia

1 Ophelia deserves to be treated like this.

2 Ophelia gives as good as she gets and really does not care for Hamlet.

3 Hamlet hates Ophelia once he realises she trusts others more than him.

4 No one else takes any notice of Hamlet teasing Ophelia; they are fascinated by the play.

5 Hamlet is cruel to Ophelia.

6 Ophelia is not quick-witted enough to defend herself against Hamlet.

7 The experience of the play is enough to make any girl lose her mind.

6 TALKING POINTS: FOUR HAMLET SOLILOQUIES

'O that ...' Talking Points

'Oh that this too too solid flesh would melt—'
(1.2, 129–58)

1 Hamlet wanted to return to his studies.

2 'Sullied' and 'solid' are interchangeable in Line 129.

3 'Solid' has resonance with four words within two lines: melt, thaw, resolve, and dew.

4 Hamlet considers suicide because he is unable to cope with the grief of losing his father.

5 He finds his mother's re-marriage disgusting in many ways.

6 The only reason Hamlet does not commit suicide is because of his religious belief.

7 He does not understand why his uncle is king.

8 He has no one to talk to about the agony he feels.

9 Hamlet believes that the marriage of Claudius and Gertrude is obviously wrong.

10 Hamlet has no thought of revenge at this point in the play, but is desperately miserable and wishes to die.

'Oh, what a rogue ...' Talking Points

'Oh, what a rogue and peasant slave am I!—'
(2.2, 508)

1 Hamlet is filled with self-loathing and distress.

2 He is not thinking straight. The actor's tears are not genuine; and his own grief is too appalling to be relieved by crying.

3 Hamlet's hatred of Claudius is more intense than he admits in his previous soliloquy.

4 He cannot understand himself.

5 Hamlet shows symptoms of clinical depression.

6 He is not mad, but may become so unless he can talk to someone.

7 Hamlet is an ordinary person, so being a murderer does not come easily, of course.

8 He is wrong to think that murder is always revealed.

9 Hamlet's wish to do something is halted by having no proof of Claudius' guilt.

10 He really does not believe that he has seen his father's ghost.

11 The idea of using the play to trap Claudius is ridiculous.

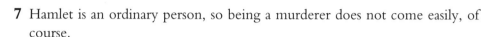

'To be ...' Talking Points

'To be, or not to be—' (3.1, 56)

1 Hamlet believes himself to be alone, but is actually being watched and listened to by Polonius, Claudius and Ophelia.

2 Hamlet answers his own question – he is religious enough to think that 'to be' is his only option.

3 Sleep is not a good analogy for death; but 'the undiscovered country' is.

4 He is so depressed that he imagines most people would prefer death to life.

5 Hamlet's description of 'life's humiliations' is surprising given that he has been brought up as a prince.

6 It is possible to think of an example from the play of each of the 'humiliations' he describes:

■ abuse from superiors;

■ insults from people who are arrogant;

■ the hurt of loving without being loved in return;

- long drawn out legal cases;

- the rudeness of those who should be helpful; and

- the way good people are wronged by those who are evil.

7 Hamlet believes that usually people put up with their lives because of fear of the unknown, or fear of change.

8 Hamlet is staying alive simply to ensure he takes revenge on Claudius.

9 His description of life as 'weary' probably rings true for many people.

10 He is right to say that thinking in depth can make you indecisive.

'How all occasions ...' Talking Points

'How all occasions do inform against me—'
(4.4, 33)

1 Hamlet is revolted by what he thinks he ought to do.

2 He thinks that human beings were made by God with a purpose in mind.

3 He thinks that people who turn away from the life set for them are no better than animals.

4 Another sort of revenge, other than murdering Claudius, would be more possible – he may have cause, will, strength and means, but he still isn't a murderer at heart.

5 Hamlet is a coward and he knows it.

6 If your honour is at stake, you should be ready to fight or die even over trivial matters.

7 'Honour' is an idea created by society for getting people to behave in certain ways.

8 The causes of Hamlet's distress – his father's death and his mother's marriage – are the reasons for his inaction, not reasons why he ought to act.

9 Soldiers fight and kill for very complex reasons; Hamlet is wrong to think that they have noble motives.

10 Hamlet tries to force himself to be a violent person; this will never work.

11 Hamlet should talk about all this with Horatio.

7 TALKING POINTS: ABOUT HAMLET'S SOLILOQUIES

1 The soliloquies indicate Hamlet's strength of character and his integrity.

2 Hamlet gives himself time to think and make decisions. This is reasonable.

3 The soliloquies show how Hamlet's resolve to act decreases over time, and how his awareness of it increases over time.

4 The chance to reflect like this has no impact on how Hamlet subsequently behaves.

5 Hamlet shows how self-indulgent he is. He could have gone to have a real talk to Ophelia, instead of talking to himself in an egotistical way – *'How all occasions do inform against me'*. This would have prevented her insanity and given him back a friend.

8 THINKING TOGETHER: HOW HAMLET FEELS

When Hamlet is talking to Horatio, we can see the sort of person he was before his father's death: amusing, friendly, open, loyal, interested and interesting. But by the start of the play, Hamlet is already damaged by events.

Clinical depression is an illness, and not the same as being 'low' or 'fed up'. Think together about what Hamlet reveals of his thoughts, and what others say about him.

Using the medical information on page 44 and your own ideas about Hamlet's state of mind revealed as he talks, discuss this Talking Point:

■ Hamlet is suffering from clinical depression

43

Clinical depression

Clinical depression is not the same as being a bit fed up. For some people, depression symptoms are so severe that it's obvious something isn't right. Other people feel generally unhappy without really knowing why. Depression symptoms vary from person to person. What has been inherited, age, gender and cultural background all play a role in how depression happens, and also in how people show that they are depressed. Depression symptoms include:

- feelings of sadness or unhappiness;

- irritability or frustration, even over small matters;

- loss of interest or pleasure in normal activities;

- reduced sex drive;

- insomnia or excessive sleeping;

- changes in appetite – decreased appetite or increased cravings for food;

- agitation or restlessness – e.g. pacing, or an inability to sit still;

- slowed thinking, speaking or body movements;

- indecisiveness, distractibility and decreased concentration;

- fatigue, tiredness and loss of energy – even small tasks may seem to require a lot of effort;

- feelings of worthlessness or guilt, fixating on past failures or blaming yourself when things aren't going right;

- trouble thinking, concentrating, making decisions and remembering;

- frequent thoughts of death, dying or suicide; and

- crying spells for no apparent reason.

9 TALKING POINTS: MISOGYNY

Misogyny: hatred, dislike, or mistrust of women.

Consider sections of the play that seem to imply misogyny in the author – or the characters. Discuss these Talking Points.

Misogyny Talking Points

1 Hamlet thinks that women are inferior to men.

2 Hamlet thinks that using make up is a sort of deception.

3 Hamlet and Horatio use the word 'woman' disparagingly.

4 Women are locked up (in a nunnery) for their own protection.

5 The links between 'honesty' and 'beauty' are hard to establish because they do not exist.

6 The idea that men should not cry is ridiculous.

7 Gertrude does little but follow Claudius about and get shouted at by Hamlet.

8 The expectation that men are always strong is an unfortunate consequence of misogyny.

9 Ophelia and Osrick have a lot in common.

References for Misogyny Talking Points

- Frailty, thy name is woman (1,2, 146)
- Painting (3,1, 143)
- Description of Gertrude in bed with Claudius (3,4, 92)
- Make up (5,1, 189)
- Duel (5,2, 209)
- Laertes (4,5, 119)
- Gertrude is to blame for everything (3,4, 89)

10 CREATE YOUR OWN *HAMLET* TALKING POINTS TO SHARE WITH OTHERS

1 Talk together to decide on a *theme* within the play.

2 Create a set of *ten Talking Points* that will help other groups to discuss your theme.

Remember that Talking Points are statements not questions. They may be considered to be 'true' or 'false'; or there may not be enough evidence to decide.

The statements should link directly to Shakespeare's text and provide an opportunity to discuss what is happening, opinions about characters and events, thoughts about relationships, or details of Shakespeare's language.

3 Share your Talking Points. Listen to the discussion of other groups.

4 Discuss Talking Points prepared by others in your class.

5 Try to give an idea of how the discussion has helped you to develop your ideas about the play.

Suggested themes for creating Talking Points

1 Revenge and justice

2 Actions and words

3 The influence of religion

4 The State of Denmark

5 Families

6 Insanity

7 Courage and cowardice

8 A character

9 Hamlet's state of mind throughout the play

11 TALKING POINTS: *HAMLET* – LANGUAGE USE DURING ACT 1 SCENE 1, 21–7

Elizabethan English can be hard to understand. Some words are unfamiliar; some word order is changed, and Shakespeare uses a range of literary techniques to increase dramatic tension, establish characters, and heighten feelings. Below are:

- Marcello's speech from Scene 1

- the *No Fear Shakespeare* version, and

- the *Hamlet Regained* version.

Read these together and discuss the Talking Points to share what you think. *(See References and links).*

Marcellus

Horatio says 'tis but our fantasy
And will not let belief take hold of him
Touching this dreaded sight twice seen of us.
Therefore I have entreated him along
With us to watch the minutes of this night,
That if again this apparition come
He may approve our eyes and speak to it.

Hamlet Regained – Marcellus

Horatio says it's only our imagination,
And refuses to believe it,
About this fearful thing we have seen twice.
Therefore, I have asked him to come along,
To keep watch with us tonight,
So if this apparition appears again,
He may agree we have seen it, and can speak to it.

***No Fear Shakespeare* – Marcellus**

Horatio says we're imagining it, and won't let himself believe anything about this horrible thing that we've seen twice now. That's why I've begged him to come on our shift tonight, so that if the Ghost appears he can see what we see and speak to it.

This version uses the following words as 'translations':

fantasy – imagination
dreaded – horrible
entreated – begged
apparition – ghost

Talking Points Act 1 Scene 1, 21–7

1 *No Fear Shakespeare* is an improvement on the original.

2 These four 'translation' words mean exactly the same as the originals.

3 Reading *No Fear Shakespeare* helps you to like Shakespeare better.

4 The *Hamlet Regained* version is more powerful than the original because it makes sense.

5 Shakespeare should never be translated like this.

6 We can create our own version of this speech that sounds more like genuine talk

7 The point of this speech is to show that Marcellus dislikes Horatio.

12 VYGOTSKY'S ESSAY ON *HAMLET*

Lev Vygotsky was a Russian psychologist whose influence on theories of education has grown steadily since the translation of his works in the 1960s. Vygotsky saw that people learn in the particular social settings they find themselves in; he realised that learning is a social activity. He saw teaching as a special sort of intervention in which a teacher could carefully support a learner through small steps of developing thinking, leaving them ultimately able to think through and complete tasks, calculations or problems alone. He showed that talk supports learning, and that talk between peers can be just as influential as talk between a teacher and a learner.

These Talking Points arise from ideas Vygotsky puts forward in his 1925 essay on Hamlet *(see References and links)*.

Talking Points: Vygotsky on *Hamlet*

1 Tolstoy said that Hamlet has no character; this lack of character is Shakespeare's intention.

2 To retell Hamlet in your own words is as impossible as putting music into words.

3 The question is not, 'Why does Hamlet delay?' but 'Why does Shakespeare make Hamlet delay?'

4 We are unable to estimate how much time elapses between the first appearance of the Ghost and the killing of the King. Is it a day, a month, a year?

5 The final scene leaves no doubt that Hamlet kills the King for his latest crimes: the poisoning of the Queen, and the killing of Laertes and Hamlet himself. Not a word is said about Hamlet's father, and the audience has completely forgotten about him.

6 The killing of the King leaves us with the feeling of duty unfulfilled, or at best, fulfilled by default.

7 The killing of the King is due to events totally beyond Hamlet's control.

8 Laertes dies inconspicuously.

9 Laertes exchanges forgiveness with Hamlet before dying. There is no apparent reason for the sudden and quite unnatural change in Laertes' character.

10 Hamlet, in his last words, points to some mysterious hidden meaning in all the preceding events.

11 Shakespeare portrayed Hamlet as a man of exceptional energy and tremendous strength, making him into a character opposite to the one actually required by the plot.

12 All the characters in the play are portrayed as Hamlet sees them.

13 We see Hamlet with Shakespeare's eyes – and Shakespeare admired Hamlet.

14 When we see the play Hamlet, we feel as if we have lived the lives of thousands of persons in one night; indeed, we have experienced more than we would have in years of common, everyday life.

13 THINKING ABOUT REVIEWS OF ACTORS PLAYING HAMLET

Thinking about actors and the most famous soliloquy

■ Use Youtube to find film clips of actors portraying the 'To be, or not to be' soliloquy.

■ Look up these actors: David Tennant: Kenneth Branagh; Richard Burton; Mel Gibson; Kevin Kline; Laurence Ollvier.

■ *See also* – Klingon Hamlet – taH Pagh taHbe'; 'You have not experienced Shakespeare until you have read him in the original Klingon,'

■ *And also* – Blackadder helps 'Bill' to edit the soliloquy. *(See References and links)*

1 Compare and evaluate the actors' performances.

2 Think about where actors pause or add emphasis to particular words and phrases. Do you think that they get it right?

3 Talk about the performances with your group to come to a decision about which actor you feel gives a performance you would like to see; and why.

Thinking about reviews of a particular performance

Talk with your group to decide if you agree or disagree with these reviews of David Tennant as Hamlet. Make sure that you can give reasons for your decision, referring to both the actor's performance, and what you know about the play. Find other reviews to add to your report back to the class. Write your own review of David Tennant's depiction of Hamlet based on the 'To be, or not to be' soliloquy.

Review 1

Tennant plays Hamlet as a raving mad man. His dignity as a prince is completely lost. He is manic and ridiculous, and his facial grimaces all but ruin every scene, making you want to laugh – or turn him off. He seems to be not really acting but just being himself. Embarrassingly bad.

Review 2

Tennant is mercurial, energetic and frantic as he tries to decide what to do. He is also thoughtful, reflective and appealing. This combination helps us to see the root causes of his indecisiveness. He brings to the character a freshness and spirit hard to portray when delivering such well-known lines.

Talking Points: *A Midsummer Night's Dream*

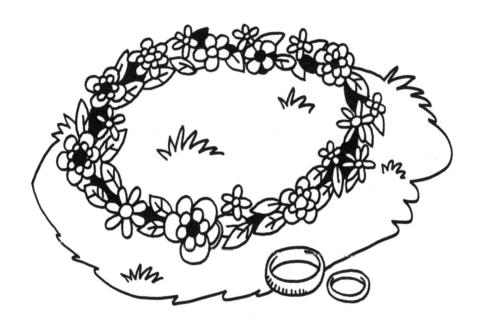

A Midsummer Night's Dream Talking Points scene by scene

A MIDSUMMER NIGHT'S DREAM TALKING POINTS: ACT 1 SCENE 1

1 We learn a lot about Theseus' character in the first act.

2 Hyppolyta is very easily pleased and a bit dull.

3 The opening scene is boring, for example compared to the beginning of Hamlet.

4 Hyppolyta and Theseus are middle aged.

5 Egeus is unimportant and only here to tell us the plot of the play.

6 Egeus' list of ways Lysander has 'bewitched' Hermia shows that Lysander has done nothing wrong.

7 Egeus is a bully.

8 Hermia is cheeky and wilful.

9 Lysander and Demetrius are very similar to one another.

10 Helena is jealous of Hermia and really dislikes her.

11 It is reckless to reveal the plan to run away, to Helena.

12 Helena's idea that 'Love looks not with the eyes, but with the mind' is right.

THINKING TOGETHER: ACT 1 SCENE 1

Hermia's father gives her three choices; marry Demetrius, become a nun or be executed. Decide together if these options are all equally dreadful. What would you do?

A MIDSUMMER NIGHT'S DREAM TALKING POINTS: ACT 1 SCENE 2

1 The change from rhymed verse in Scene 1 to prose in Scene 2 is important.

2 Quince is the leader of the group.

3 Quince knows how to manage Bottom.

4 Snug cannot read.

5 The mechanicals get it into their heads that if Lion frightens the ladies they will be hanged.

6 The play is designed to contain characters like the young lovers Hermia and Lysander.

THINKING TOGETHER: ACT 1 SCENE 2

Discuss and draw the six mechanicals in their usual dress, and their play costumes.

A MIDSUMMER NIGHT'S DREAM TALKING POINTS: ACT 2 SCENE 1

1 The move to the wood is important for the plot of the play.

2 Puck and the Fairy have never met before.

3 The Fairy dislikes Puck because of what he does.

4 Puck's account of himself is self indulgent; the Fairy reveals his darker side.

5 Titania is furious because Oberon has been unfaithful to her.

6 Oberon reveals that Theseus is not the gentleman he appeared to be in Act 1.

7 Titania's list of 'things that are wrong' sound like the effects of climate change.

8 The little human boy is Titania's responsibility.

9 Oberon only wants charge of the boy because Titania won't release him.

10 The row between Titania and Oberon is irrelevant to the plot.

11 Titania and Oberon are equally powerful.

12 Puck does not really know why Oberon sends him for the flower.

13 The flower is the link between humans and fairies.

14 'Love-in-idleness' is what we now call Heartsease or wild pansy.

15 Oberon is unscrupulous and used to getting his own way.

16 Helena makes a fool of herself and you can see why Demetrius despises her.

THINKING TOGETHER: ACT 2 SCENE 1

Titania Sleeps: Decide together how you could animate or dramatise the description Oberon gives of where Titania sleeps, and how he drops juice from the flower into her eyes.

A MIDSUMMER NIGHT'S DREAM TALKING POINTS: ACT 2 SCENE 2

1 Oberon's words as he puts juice in Titania's eyes are a spell.

2 Puck makes an honest mistake.

3 Lysander's speech to Helena is plausible and yet does not quite ring true.

4 Hermia is afraid of the dark.

THINKING TOGETHER: ACT 2 SCENE 2

Discuss and create stage directions for this scene. Think about each character and where they need to be at the start of the scene, when they are on stage, when they are speaking and how they leave the stage. Use your stage directions to make this scene really dramatic. Think about the placing and use of different exits and entrances. Include details about what props and lighting you would use to bring the scene to life.

A MIDSUMMER NIGHT'S DREAM TALKING POINTS: ACT 3 SCENE 1

1 The characters are described as 'clowns', which influences how we think of them.

2 Bottom is determined to be the star of the show.

3 Bottom's suggestions are all accepted without question by the group.

4 Puck picks on Bottom because he is so ridiculous.

5 Bottom is bewildered by the way his friends treat him.

6 Puck is invisible to humans, and only Bottom can see the fairies.

7 The fairies take no notice of anything Bottom says.

8 Even with the spell, Titania is horrified by Bottom's voice – or what he says.

A MIDSUMMER NIGHT'S DREAM TALKING POINTS: ACT 3 SCENE 2

1 Puck acts as a jester for Oberon, entertaining him by dramatising the story of Titania and Bottom.

2 Helena is completely confused by Lysander's change of heart.

3 Helena is convinced that both men are being cruel to her.

4 Some truths about Helena and Hermia's friendship surface as they argue.

5 The scene has the characteristics of a bad dream for both Helena and Hermia.

6 Oberon is angry with Puck.

7 Oberon is selfish and controlling; despite everything he continues his quest to take the boy from Titania.

8 Puck always obeys Oberon.

9 Puck does not really regret having interfered with the humans.

A MIDSUMMER NIGHT'S DREAM TALKING POINTS: ACT 4 SCENE 1

1 Bottom shows that he is courteous and charming.

2 Oberon is ashamed of himself.

3 Oberon thinks Titania is easy to control.

4 Titania changes her mind and is happy to let the child go to Oberon.

5 Puck is right to have a low opinion of Bottom.

6 Thesus is convinced that he can impress Hyppolyta with his hunting hounds.

7 Hyppolyta is haughty and a bit of a show-off.

8 Theseus is one of those people who only really think of themselves.

9 Theseus and Hyppolyta are shocked to find the lovers together.

10 Lysander, half asleep, tells the truth – a dangerous thing to do.

11 Egeus is an aggressive, bullying person and hates Theseus for over-ruling him.

12 Demetrius finally comes to his senses.

13 There is little difference between Helena and Hermia, Demetrius and Lysander.

14 Theseus is tolerant of the young people but we don't know why.

15 Bottom's speech is confused and unintelligent.

16 Bottom's dream was reality while it was happening.

17 Bottom is thinking of Thisbe when he talks of 'her death' .

A MIDSUMMER NIGHT'S DREAM TALKING POINTS: ACT 4 SCENE 2

1 'Confusion' is a good word to sum up the feelings of Bottom's friends.

2 Snug shows how divided the classes of people are; he does not know Hermia and friends.

3 The Players are angry with Bottom, because they thought that the play would make them wealthy.

4 Bottom appears as if from the dead and sorts out all their worries.

A MIDSUMMER NIGHT'S DREAM TALKING POINTS: ACT 5 SCENE 1

1 Theseus who is part of an 'antique fable' finds such things incredible.

2 He describes how Shakespeare thinks of writing.

3 Theseus contrasts *reason* and *imagination* in a rather crude way.

4 Imagination is essential for all of us to create our own lives.

5 Imagination depends on the context we find ourselves in.

6 Hyppolyta believes in magic.

7 Philostrate is patronising and officious.

8 Philostrate has seen the play so knows what it is like.

9 Philostrate thinks the only amusement to be had from the play will be to laugh at the Players.

10 Thesus' idea of 'simpleness and duty' shows that he is used to people being subservient.

11 Hyppolyta thinks the play might be boring, or upsetting, or embarrassing.

12 Theseus thinks that he ought to be kind although he agrees that the play will be ridiculous.

13 Theseus is in a good mood and up for anything.

14 Theseus is sensitive to the impact of his patronage on the less well off.

15 He likes it when people are over-awed by his presence.

16 He thinks Hyppolyta talks too much.

17 As the play begins, Quince is scared stiff!

18 Bottom is nervous and this makes him garrulous.

19 His words all come out wrong.

20 The play is brilliantly funny.

21 Bottom can't stay in role. He is irritating.

22 Hyppoltya whinges all the way through the play. She is haughty and bad-tempered.

23 Thisbe's final speech is genuinely moving.

24 Throughout this scene, Lysander and Demetrius
    show an easy friendship with Theseus.

25 Lysander and Demetrius think they are witty, but
    they are not.

26 Theseus really loves the play.

27 Puck's list of things that mean 'night' needs updating.

28 Titania and Oberon are determined that other couples should be happy,
    now they are.

29 Puck has heard the idea that players are 'like shadows' before.

30 Puck wrongly confuses shadows with images from dreams.

31 Puck apologises for the entire play – this is what Shakespeare himself
    wanted to do.

More Thinking Together for *A Midsummer Night's Dream*

1 THINKING ABOUT THESEUS

Theseus was the mythical founder and King of the Greek city of Athens.

Some of Theseus' adventures

Adapted from the work of the Greek writer Plutarch (AD 46–AD 120)

Theseus fought at the battle of the Lapithae against the Centaurs. Also, he helped Adrastus, King of the Argives, to recover the bodies of those that were killed in the battle at the city of Thebes.

Theseus, on his journey across Greece, came across and conquered many villains. One of these was Sinnis. Sinnis had a beautiful daughter called Periguna, who fled when she saw her father killed in battle. But Theseus saw her, and followed her. She hid in a grove of a kind of wild prickly bushes called *stoebe*. Frightened, and acting like a child, she entreated the bushes to hide her, as if they could hear. But Theseus found her and called to her; he swore that he would be kind to her and that he would not hurt her or do anything to distress her. Believing his promises, she came out of the bushes.

Later, after Theseus arrived in Crete, he slew the monster (half-man, half beast) called the Minotaur, with the help of Ariadne. Ariadne, being in love with him, gave him the clue that would save his life; she gave him thread to make his way out of the Minotaur's labyrinth or maze, so that he returned the same way he went in. Ariadne fell further in love with Theseus, seeing him as good, strong and invincible in wrestling.

After this, Theseus left Ariadne heartbroken because he had fallen in love with the nymph Aegles, the daughter of Panopeus. On a sea voyage, he went with Hercules to war against the Amazons. The Amazons were a tribe of fierce warrior women who killed all their boy children. Theseus enticed Antiopa the Amazon to come on to his ship. He invited her on board. She accepted, bringing with her a present; but as soon as she was aboard, he hoisted his sail, and carried her away. After this kidnapping it took four months until peace was restored between the Amazons and the Athenians. The peace-maker was one of the Amazonian women called Hyppolyta. Theseus married Hyppolyta.

- Discuss who or what your group would like to research: *Centaurs, Theseus, Hyppolyta, Antiopa, Aegles, Ariadne, Minotaur, Hercules, Amazon women, Plutarch, Athens, Mazes.*

- Carry out your research with your group.

- Prepare a presentation for the class. Alternatively, dramatise the story you find.

2 THINKING ABOUT TITANIA AND OBERON

Thinking Together: The quarrel

Here is the exchange Titania and Oberon have about Theseus and Hyppolyta's past – and their own:

Titania
Why art thou here,
Come from the farthest Steppe of India?
But that, forsooth, the bouncing Amazon,
Your buskin'd mistress and your warrior love,
To Theseus must be wedded, and you come
To give their bed joy and prosperity.

Oberon
How canst thou thus for shame, Titania,
Glance at my credit with Hippolyta,
Knowing I know thy love to Theseus?
Didst thou not lead him through the glimmering night
From Perigenia, whom he ravished?
And make him with fair Aegle break his faith,
With Ariadne and Antiopa?

Think together to:

- match up what Titania says with Hyppolyta's story;

- match up what Oberon says with Theseus' story.

In groups of three, role play this scenario

One of you is a relationships ('marriage guidance') counsellor. The other two play Titania and Oberon.

Titania and Oberon's relationship is in trouble and they have arrived to discuss what is going wrong with the counsellor.

Create the scene, starting with the exchange of angry words above. Decide what the counsellor should say. What should this couple be encouraged to talk about – jealousy, the past, anger, lies, exaggerations, unkindness, unrealistic expectations? Perhaps the disputed child is brought into the story. Your scene could be serious or a comedy.

Be ready to present your scene for the rest of the class.

3 TALKING POINTS: THE SCIENCE OF MIDSUMMER

'Midsummer' is the time around the summer solstice. The summer solstice is the day of the year when there is most daylight – the 'longest day', June 21 in the northern hemisphere. It has traditionally been celebrated by holidays, festivals and rituals.

Think about the solar system and the earth's movement in space. Discuss these Talking Points to come to an agreement to share with the class. Are these Talking Points *true* or *false* – or are you *unsure*? What are your reasons?

The science of midsummer: Talking Points

1 Night and day are caused by the rotation of the earth.

2 The longest day is the same length in time as all other days.

3 The Earth rotates around the sun in an almost circular orbit.

4 The summer solstice is the day of the year with the longest daylight.

5 In the northern hemisphere, some places have daylight 24 hours a day in summer.

6 The seasons of the year are caused by the way the earth is tilted on its axis.

7 The earth tips over so that we in the north face the sun more in summer.

8 The earth moves around the sun at the same angle all the time.

9 The sun reaches its highest position in the sky on the day of the summer solstice.

10 When it's midsummer night here, it's midwinter night in Antarctica.

11 Solstice celebrations are about appreciating the sun as source of light and energy.

12 There is more light and heat on midsummer night than any other night of the year.

13 The word *solstice* comes from Latin *sol* (sun) and *sistere* (to stand still).

14 Stonehenge is an ancient stone temple dedicated to sun worship.

15 The solstice is the beginning of the end of summer.

16 It's very rare to have a full moon at the summer solstice.

17 A full moon happens when no clouds cover the moon.

18 The moon changes shape randomly, to do with gravity and the tides of the sea.

19 The moon changes shape because it casts a shadow on itself.

20 The play could be set at any time of year – 'midsummer' is irrelevant.

Talking Points:
Romeo and Juliet

Romeo and Juliet
Talking Points scene
by scene

1 The rivalry between the Montagues and Capulets is continued only by the men of the families.

2 The Prince is angry mainly because the two families have caused other street fights recently.

3 The Prince thinks that making threats will end the violence; but this will not be effective for long.

4 Benvolio gives a truthful account of what started the fight.

5 Romeo's mother thinks that he needs to be protected from the world.

6 Romeo has fallen in love with an older woman who does not really like him.

7 Tybalt calls Benvolio a coward; he is right.

8 Romeo would be happier if he took up sport or spent time studying – he is just bored.

THINKING TOGETHER: ACT 1 SCENE 1

■ Draw a cartoon of Romeo.

■ Annotate the picture with all the *opposites* that Romeo uses as he talks to Benvolio (lines 161–86). Decide on a sentence that sums up Romeo's state of mind at this point in time. Think up a conversation you might have with him, to find out if he agrees with your idea.

ROMEO AND JULIET TALKING POINTS: ACT 1 SCENES 2, 3 AND 4

1 Romeo has a crush on Rosaline, who is Juliet's cousin. Benvolio persuades him to gate-crash the Capulet's party so that he can see other attractive girls, and forget her.

2 Juliet is thirteen years old.

3 Juliet's father does not want her to be married because he likes her company.

4 Juliet's mother wants her to be married so that she will have a rich husband.

5 Benvolio thinks that if he, Romeo and Mercutio join in the dancing at the party, they are less likely to be noticed.

6 Romeo does not want to attend the party because he is not a sociable person.

THINKING TOGETHER: ACT 1 SCENE 4

■ Share ideas about Mercutio's image of Queen Mab, bringer of dreams.

■ Draw her and annotate your picture with words from Mercutio's description.

■ Draw a cartoon, story board or graphics to show scenes he describes to Romeo and Benvolio.

ROMEO AND JULIET TALKING POINTS: ACT 1 SCENE 5

1 The instant Romeo sees Juliet, he completely forgets Rosaline.

2 Capulet is surprisingly tolerant of Romeo's presence at the party. This is because he has been warned by the Prince to avoid arguments with the Montagues.

3 It is reasonable for Tybalt to want to fight Romeo, because he has been brought up to consider Montagues as villains and enemies.

4 Romeo and Juliet's first conversation with each other is a sonnet *(lines 93–106)*.

5 Romeo would act this way with any beautiful girl.

6 Juliet is not surprised when Romeo kisses her.

7 Both Romeo and Juliet ask the Nurse about one another; the Nurse does not understand the importance of the questions.

8 Romeo uses the word 'foe'; Juliet used the word 'enemy'; both are afraid of what has happened.

9 It would be sensible for Romeo or Juliet – or both – to put their family loyalty before their new infatuation.

THINKING TOGETHER: ACT 1 SCENE 5

Work together to create a time-line for the play, starting with the servants Sampson and Gregory fighting. The Capulet's party is the same evening. Record on your time-line what Juliet, Romeo and Tybalt do on this first day. Leave space for the evening, when Romeo will meet Juliet again secretly . . .

ROMEO AND JULIET TALKING POINTS: ACT 2 SCENES 1 AND 2

1 Mercutio sees Romeo as young, silly and easily infatuated.

2 Benvolio is a better person than Mercutio.

3 Romeo's romantic ideas about Juliet are all to do with light and space.

4 Romeo would rather just watch Juliet than speak with her.

5 Juliet is already willing to shake off her family ties for Romeo.

6 Juliet is afraid; more afraid for Romeo than pleased to see him.

7 Juliet is embarrassed because Romeo overheard her.

8 She knows that it is not sensible to be too honest about feelings like love.

9 The idea of marriage is Juliet's; she knows that unless she acts quickly, her family will marry her to Paris.

10 Romeo is looking for romance, but impulsively accepts the idea of marriage.

11 They have little to say to one another, but find it hard to part.

12 Romeo is unable to keep his new love affair secret. Talking about it is part of the charm.

THINKING TOGETHER: ACT 2 SCENES 1 AND 2

■ Complete the time-line by adding a brief summary of the events of day one.

■ Imagine that Romeo and Juliet had mobile phones. Instead of meeting, they send texts. Write the texts that they exchange after the party and before Romeo leaves.

71

ROMEO AND JULIET TALKING POINTS: ACT 2 SCENE 3

1 The Friar is old and confused.

2 His view of people is that good and bad exist in everyone, but that evil brings death.

3 Rhyme helps the Friar's words to carry some authority.

4 He treats Romeo in a patronising manner.

5 The Friar is astonished at Romeo's rapid change of heart, and finds him ridiculous.

6 Romeo would just have readily married Rosaline if she had returned his love.

7 The Friar is right. 'Love' for Romeo means a big emotional response to a girl's looks.

8 The Friar believes that marriage between Capulet and Montague might unite the families; but he does not think straight, and makes the fatal error of helping Romeo keep it all secret.

9 The Friar's views, that good and evil co-exist, and that when you rush you get things wrong, are generally true, but not always.

10 Romeo is in a real hurry; it is hard to say quite why.

THINKING TOGETHER: ACT 2 SCENE 3

Start a time-line for the events of day two. Keep adding events as they happen until the end of the day.

ROMEO AND JULIET TALKING POINTS: ACT 2 SCENE 4

1 Tybalt, angry because Romeo came to his home, has challenged him to fight.

2 Romeo would not stand a chance in a swordfight with Tybalt.

3 Mercutio is opinionated and wordy, but he cares for Romeo.

4 Romeo is very innocent and does not understand what Mercutio implies.

5 Romeo is noticeably happier; he is witty and sharp; his friends are pleased.

6 Romeo is showing off, and is rude to the Nurse.

7 The Nurse misuses some important words.

8 Romeo and the Nurse do not really trust one another.

9 The Nurse makes no attempt to stop the marriage.

10 She is acting as go-between, for the money.

11 The Nurse tells Romeo about Paris to make him even more eager to marry.

12 Being in Juliet's confidence makes the Nurse feel important for once.

ROMEO AND JULIET TALKING POINTS: ACT 2 SCENE 5

1 Juliet's mind is full of ideas about time.

2 At heart, she despises the Nurse.

3 The Nurse's ideas of her own importance are gaining ground.

4 The Nurse and Juliet are equally grumpy, for different reasons.

5 Marriage is more interesting to Juliet than Romeo himself.

6 The Nurse shows she can be equally as offensive as Mercutio.

7 Juliet is both delighted and frightened by the wedding plan.

ROMEO AND JULIET TALKING POINTS: ACT 2 SCENE 6

1 The Friar gives Romeo some good advice.

2 Romeo's ideas about the consequences of his actions are irresponsible.

3 At this, their third meeting, Romeo and Juliet are at their happiest so far.

4 The Friar is a little horrified by the extreme nature of their passion.

ROMEO AND JULIET TALKING POINTS: ACT 3 SCENE 1

1 Benvolio is a sensible person.

2 Mercutio's account of Benvolio is fictional or, at least, exaggerated.

3 Mercutio is drunk and aggressive towards his friend and his enemy.

4 Mercutio thinks that Romeo is taunting Tybalt.

5 Mercutio starts the fight.

6 Mercutio is wounded because of Romeo's interference.

7 At this instant, both Tybalt and Mercutio know Mercutio is fatally wounded.

8 Romeo cannot take responsibility and blames Juliet.

9 Tybalt comes back because he wants to apologise.

10 Romeo is a brilliant swordsman, and he is also furiously angry.

11 Tybalt's death is more important to Romeo than Mercutio's.

12 Benvolio gives an accurate account of events.

13 Lady Capulet is hysterical and mindlessly vengeful.

14 The Prince ignores the idea that Romeo tried to avoid a fight.

15 Romeo should be executed for the death of Tybalt.

THINKING TOGETHER: ACT 3 SCENE 1

1   Draw a plan of the market square in Verona.
    Make counters or images for all the people
    who speak in this scene and the other men
    present. Set them out as the scene starts.
    Move them through the scene, marking
    movement, important events and words on
    your plan. Add times for each event.

2   The Prince enters with both Montague and
    Capulet and their wives. Where did they
    come from? Why are they all together?
    What were they doing or talking about?
    Devise a scene that shows what your group
    thinks was happening before the families
    were called to the market place.

ROMEO AND JULIET TALKING POINTS: ACT 3 SCENE 2

1 Juliet is still wishing her life away.

2 Now that she is married, she is calmer.

3 She imagines losing her virginity.

4 Juliet has had to live a very boring life and now she can see an escape.

5 Her ideas are immature; she feels as a child would before a party.

6 She thinks Romeo is dead and is furious with the Nurse.

7 The Nurse cares nothing for Tybalt and is not that fond of Juliet, but likes a drama.

8 Juliet is distraught because Romeo is banished.

9 She threatens suicide.

10 The Nurse has no proof that Romeo is with the Friar.

ROMEO AND JULIET TALKING POINTS: ACT 3 SCENE 3

1 Romeo's thoughts about being *banished* echo Juliet's response to the word.

2 Romeo feels massively sorry for himself.

3 Romeo talks nonsense; he is simply whingeing.

4 The Friar does not understand how Romeo feels.

5 The Friar is afraid of the Prince.

6 The Nurse's comparison of Romeo's state with Juliet's embarrasses him.

7 Romeo trusts the Friar to stop him killing himself.

8 The Friar talks some sense into Romeo.

9 Romeo is so eager to see Juliet on their wedding night that he is easily persuaded to go.

10 Romeo trusts the Friar and the Nurse.

ROMEO AND JULIET TALKING POINTS: ACT 3 SCENE 4

1 Juliet's parents are more concerned to marry her off than they are about Tybalt's death.

2 Capulet is bossy and arrogant.

3 Two days is long enough to show respect for the dead.

4 Juliet's parents want her married for her own safety.

5 Paris does not care what Juliet thinks.

6 Capulet finds talk of weddings boring and simply wants it over with.

ROMEO AND JULIET TALKING POINTS: ACT 3 SCENE 5

1 Romeo is so much in love with Juliet that she can persuade him that day is night.

2 Juliet's love for Romeo means she readily forgives him for killing Tybalt.

3 Romeo is feeling much more optimistic this morning.

4 Juliet wants to keep the drama going and will not be reassured.

5 Tragically they part in a real hurry.

6 Lady Capulet is all talk and will not really plan to murder Romeo.

7 Juliet nearly gives the truth away in her talk of Romeo.

8 She is appalled by the idea of a hasty marriage to Paris.

9 Lady Capulet is an evil person.

10 Capulet is a tyrant and his attitude to Juliet is cruel.

11 Lady Capulet fears for herself because Juliet has put Capulet in a rage.

12 The Nurse does not mean what she says.

13 Juliet is not quick-witted, but she suddenly realises she must make her own decisions.

ROMEO AND JULIET TALKING POINTS: ACT 4 SCENE 1

1 The Friar is dishonest with Paris.

2 Juliet's dismissal of Paris is impressive.

3 Paris is not a bad person, just insensitive – and in love.

4 The Friar is keen to give his sleeping potion a try.

5 Juliet does not ask any questions; this is foolish.

6 Juliet is alone, and her only strength lies in thinking of Romeo.

7 Romeo ought to be part of this conversation but has gone to Mantua.

ROMEO AND JULIET TALKING POINTS: ACT 4 SCENE 2

1 Juliet is very good at deception; or, she is desperate and acts accordingly.

2 The Nurse completely believes Juliet's change of heart.

3 Juliet hates her mother and father.

4 Capulet is only happy when he is getting his own way.

5 He brings the wedding forward a day because he does not trust Juliet.

6 If Juliet had not met Romeo, she would have been happy with Paris.

ROMEO AND JULIET TALKING POINTS: ACT 4 SCENE 3

1 Juliet is very afraid of the potion.

2 She tries to trust the Friar, but at heart does not.

3 Her description of the Capulet vault is truly fearful.

4 She has visited the vault so knows what it is like.

5 Juliet is more afraid of the tomb than of the potion.

6 In the end, she drinks in a kind of distracted nightmare.

ROMEO AND JULIET TALKING POINTS: ACT 4 SCENE 4

1 Paris arrives at Capulet's far too early.

2 The Nurse sees Juliet only as a plaything for Paris.

3 Capulet and Lady Capulet talk a lot about grief, but it is all talk.

4 The Friar is always claiming that things are for the best, as he does here.

5 No one suggests that Juliet has killed herself.

6 Her family believe Juliet died of grief over Tybalt.

7 Peter is the only person who shows real sorrow.

8 Music can help where words cannot.

9 The musicians can play healing music; but they are rude and callous men.

ROMEO AND JULIET TALKING POINTS: ACT 5 SCENE 1

1 Romeo has slept well, so he is in a good mood.

2 Hearing the news of Juliet, he asks his servant no questions; this is unwise.

3 Romeo knows that the Friar has instructions for him, but chooses to ignore this.

4 Romeo has already thought of buying poison – this is a plan he has made earlier.

5 It is surprising that he knows an Apothecary in Mantua.

6 The Apothecary does not want to give out poison.

7 He is easily bought, as anyone who is starving and needs money would be.

ROMEO AND JULIET TALKING POINTS: ACT 5 SCENE 2

1 Friar John did not take the job of delivering the letter seriously.

2 He makes an excuse for not delivering the letter.

3 Friar Lawrence realises that Juliet will be afraid in the tomb, and rushes to help her.

4 He writes to Romeo again before he goes to the Capulet tomb.

ROMEO AND JULIET TALKING POINTS: ACT 5 SCENE 3

1 Paris visits Juliet's grave to grieve alone; he really did love her.

2 Romeo is raging and angry; his servant is afraid of him.

3 Balthasar intends to help Romeo if he can.

4 Romeo wants to see Juliet and to wear the ring she wears.

5 Paris has no idea what Romeo is doing at the tomb.

6 Paris knows Romeo can fight brilliantly but will not leave as asked; he shows courage.

7 Romeo does not know who he is fighting with.

8 Romeo fears leaving Juliet alone in the tomb.

9 He knows that with both Tybalt and Paris dead, he will be killed by the Capulets.

10 He thinks of nothing but Juliet as he dies.

11 The Friar and the servant are both cowards.

12 Juliet does not even consider the Friar's plan for her.

13 The first people on the scene cannot understand what has happened.

14 The Friar does not give a completely truthful account of events.

15 The Prince collects all the important evidence.

16 He blames the families, not the Friar.

17 The tragic ending makes thoughts of revenge or justice pointless.

More Thinking Together for *Romeo and Juliet*

1 ROMEO: THINKING TOGETHER

The following activities look at Romeo's ideas when he is alone. Work with a group to think about the text and your ideas about Romeo.

Thinking Together: Act 1 Scene 1, 161–73

1   Think together to make up the dialogue Romeo had with Rosaline, during which he finds out that she has taken a vow of chastity. Perhaps they are talking on the phone or by email.

2   Print a copy of Romeo's speech beginning '*Alas that love, whose view is muffled still*' and illustrate with cartoons that show the things he describes in terms of opposites.

3   Think of a set of adjectives you would use to describe first impressions of Romeo at this point in the play.

4   Design Romeo's bedroom. You need to think about what music he should listen to, what posters would be on the walls – who are his heroes, what sort of clothes he might wear, what things he likes having about.

Thinking Together: Act 2 Scene 2, 2–25

Romeo is completely taken by Juliet; think of a set of adjectives to describe Romeo at this stage in the play, and add to your list from Act 1.

Thinking Together: Act 3 Scene 3, 29–51

1   Romeo thinks that suicide would be a better option than being banished. He thinks with jealousy of the lowly creatures who can look at and be near Juliet. Draw a cartoon of Juliet with the creatures, and Romeo in exile, adding your words to bring it to life.

2   Romeo cannot bear the idea of being *banished*; he uses the word with horror over and over again. Make a list of every time Romeo uses the word 'banished' or 'exile' with a note of exactly what his ideas are about banishment, for each time he says the word.

   What is your own experience of being banished; can you share it, to better understand how he feels?

Thinking Together: Act 5 Scene 1, 1–17 and 36–59

1   Draw Romeo's dream.

2   Write the letter Romeo writes to his father.

3   Draw and annotate the inside of the apothecary's shop, and the apothecary himself, using Romeo's words.

4   Add to your list of adjectives describing Romeo. Say how you think of him at this stage in the play.

Thinking Together: Act 5 Scene 3, 82–125

1   Romeo has killed Tybalt, betrayed his family by marrying secretly, disobeyed the Friar and broken the law laid down by the Prince, threatened his servant and killed Count Paris. Think about what he says in his last words. Say what you think he regrets; what is he happy about; why exactly he kills himself; and what you think of him as a person.

2   Imagine that either Mercutio or Benvolio came along to the tomb while Romeo is considering taking the poison. Make up their dialogue with Romeo; what would be the outcome?

3 Add a final set of adjectives to say how you see Romeo. Look at all the adjectives you have collected. Think together to write an epitaph for Romeo from the point of view of the Friar; his mother; Bonvolio; Balthasar, or Juliet.

2 JULIET: THINKING TOGETHER

Juliet – Talking Points

1 Juliet is obedient, wilful, determined, strong and brave.

2 Juliet is admirable.

3 Juliet is a spoilt, bad tempered girl who caused her own destruction.

Juliet and her parents – Talking Points

Act 1 Scene 2; Act 3 Scene 5

1 Capulet believes that Juliet is far too young to marry.

2 Capulet realises that Paris is 'a good catch' for Juliet.

3 Capulet does not understand Juliet.

4 Capulet is bossy and domineering – or protective and sensible.

5 Lady Capulet resents Juliet's youth and freedom.

6 Lady Capulet wants to see Juliet married off; it doesn't matter who to.

7 Lady Capulet allows her husband to dominate the household.

8 Lady Capulet is cruel and controlling – or weak and a bit of a bully.

9 Juliet admires her parents – till she meets Romeo.

10 Capulet means every word he says to Juliet.

11 Capulet's decision to bring forward the wedding to Paris causes Juliet's death.

12 Capulet knows it was his fault.

13 Faced with Juliet's death, Lady Capulet thinks only of herself.

Juliet talks to Romeo – Talking Points

Act 1 Scene 5; Act 2 Scene 2; Act 2 Scene 6; Act 3 Scene 5; Act 5 Scene 3

1 Juliet and Romeo understand one another from their first words together.

2 At their second meeting, Juliet, having declared her love, is honest with Romeo.

3 Juliet is confident enough to believe that Romeo loves her.

4 Juliet assumes that Romeo wants to marry her.

5 Juliet does all the planning for their next meeting.

6 At their third meeting, the Friar does not even try to talk Juliet out of a hasty marriage.

7 Juliet's idea that love is wealth is inappropriate.

8 On their wedding night together, they are truly happy.

9 They treat one another as trusted friends as well as lovers.

10 Juliet is reassured by Romeo's optimism as they part.

11 Juliet refuses to leave the tomb because she has seen Romeo.

12 She has no hesitation in dying once convinced that he is dead.

Juliet alone – Talking Points

Act 2 Scene 5

1 Juliet's scathing comments about her Nurse are childish.

2 Juliet does not trust her Nurse.

3 Juliet knows that her Nurse is more loyal to her family than to herself personally.

Act 3 Scene 2

1 Juliet is still raging against the slow (that is, normal) passing of time.

2 Juliet is slightly afraid of the night ahead.

3 Juliet hopes that the night will hide some aspects of their love.

4 She thinks that love will be what makes the difference.

5 Juliet wishes that Romeo – as little stars – will be her personal heaven.

6 Juliet sees herself as having outgrown childish things now.

Act 3 Scene 5, 236–44

1 Juliet is completely astonished by the Nurse's change of mind.

2 Juliet must have experienced the Nurse behaving in this way many times.

3 She does not even consider doing as the Nurse says.

4 What the Nurse has said to her is probably true.

5 Fear and anger help her to be deceptive.

6 With Romeo in exile, the Friar is now the only person to rely on.

7 It is not a good idea to rely on the Friar.

Act 5 Scene 3

1 Juliet has no regret in saying goodbye to her mother and Nurse.

2 She is strong enough to act alone, and she knows it.

3 She really does not trust the Friar.

4 She is terrified of the dark.

5 The idea of seeing Tybalt's corpse is enough to scare anyone.

6 She imagines that Romeo will be in danger.

7 Juliet has no choice but to drink the sleeping potion.

Act 5 Scene 3, 173–80

1 Juliet realises that the Friar, too, has let her down.

2 She has seen Romeo, so refuses to leave the tomb.

3 She is almost angry with Romeo.

4 She could at this point tell the truth and expect some sympathy from her family.

5 Her death by suicide takes more bravery than Romeo's.

6 Juliet believes that there is an afterlife in which she will be happy.

3 THINKING TOGETHER: TIME-LINE FOR *ROMEO AND JULIET*

Using the play text, talk with your group to complete this time-line for Romeo and Juliet. Say what happens at each of the times detailed.

Day 1: Sunday

Street fight between –

Romeo goes to the Capulet's party. Romeo and Juliet meet and:

First meeting – at the party –

Second meeting – after the party –

Day 2: Monday

Morning:

Romeo sees Friar Lawrence to –

Romeo and Mercutio tease the Nurse who comes to arrange Romeo's –

Juliet visits the Friar – third meeting –

Mid afternoon:

A fight in which Tybalt –

Then Romeo –

Romeo's punishment is –

Late evening:

Nurse visits Romeo and they arrange –

Capulet arranges to –

Day 3: Tuesday

Romeo and Juliet's fourth meeting –

Romeo goes –

Lady Capulet tells Juliet –

Capulet –

The Nurse –

Juliet meets Paris at Friar Lawrence's cell; he gives Juliet –

She goes home and –

Capulet –

Alone, Juliet –

Day 4: Wednesday

Paris arrives at Capulet's to find –

Romeo is told of Juliet's death and –

Friar Lawrence finds out that –

Friar Lawrence sets off to –

Romeo meets and kills –

Romeo sees Juliet for the fifth time and –

Juliet awakes with the Friar present. He leaves –

The Watch –

The Prince –

Montague and Capulet –

4 THINKING TOGETHER: GROUP RESEARCH INTO KEY THEMES

This is an opportunity to research a theme from *Romeo and Juliet*, in depth.

- First choose which of the areas below interests your group most.

- Discuss ideas to decide what aspects of the theme you will look at.

- Find out as much as you can, keeping a record of the sources you use.

- Discuss your research findings.

- Prepare a presentation in which each one of you takes a part in communicating your ideas.

Topics for research

1 Shakespeare used several sources for *Romeo and Juliet*.

2 *Romeo and Juliet* can be staged in lots of different ways.

3 The 'Chorus' is pointless and gives away the plot unnecessarily.

4 *Romeo and Juliet* is not a tragedy.

5 Juliet is much more interesting and believable than Ophelia.

6 Queen Mab is the Celtic fairy associated with dreams. After *Romeo and Juliet*, many other authors were inspired by Queen Mab stories.

7 Romeo and Juliet influence and decide on their own fate; there is no such thing as destiny.

8 The Montagues are better parents than the Capulets.

9 In Shakespeare's plays, a Clown is a servant, uneducated, and easily ridiculed.

10 Love in *Romeo and Juliet* is a mixture of magic and something like religion.

11 *Romeo and Juliet* was written by Shakespeare when he was 26 years old – about the same age as Lady Capulet and Juliet's Nurse. Yet the characters in the play all behave like people who are much older.

---

5 THINKING TOGETHER: MERCUTIO, ROMEO'S COUSIN

In J.D. Salinger's *The Catcher in the Rye*, Holden Caulfield is at Grand Central station (New York) where he strikes up a conversation with a nun he sits next to in a sandwich bar. She asks him what books he has read and he mentions Romeo and Juliet; he says he liked it, but not some things about it. She asks him to say what he means.

> 'Well, I'm not too crazy about Romeo and Juliet,' I said. 'I mean I like them, but – I don't know. They get pretty annoying sometimes. I mean I felt much sorrier when old Mercutio got killed than when Romeo and Juliet did. The thing is, I never liked Romeo too much after Mercutio gets stabbed by that other man – Juliet's cousin – what's his name?'
>
> 'Tybalt.'
>
> 'That's right, Tybalt,' I said – I always forget that guy's name. 'It was Romeo's fault. I mean, I liked him the best in the play, old Mercutio. All those Montagues and Capulets, they're all right – especially Juliet – but Mercutio, he was – it's hard to explain. He was very smart and entertaining and all. The thing is, it drives me crazy if somebody gets killed – especially somebody very smart and entertaining and all – and it's somebody else's fault. Romeo and Juliet, at least it was their own fault.'
>
> From *The Catcher in the Rye*, J.D. Salinger

1   Talk together to work out exactly what Holden thinks of the play and the characters he mentions. Decide whether or not you agree with what he says about Romeo, Juliet and Mercutio – with reasons for your ideas; and who is to blame for their deaths.

   Think about why he forgets Tybalt's name.

   Think about why Holden hates it so much if 'somebody gets killed . . . and it's somebody else's fault'.

2   Use the play text to say why Holden thinks of Mercutio as 'smart' and 'entertaining'.

3   Imagine that Holden and Mercutio meet in the sandwich bar at the station. Make up their conversation about Romeo.

4   Mercutio is clever, witty and reckless. Imagine that he still lives, and in the final scene of the play accompanies Romeo to the graveyard, where they meet Paris. What happens? Can you write an ending to the play that you all agree on?

6 THINKING TOGETHER: TYBALT, JULIET'S COUSIN

Tybalt 'Prince of Cats' is named after the Tibert, the King's Messenger, in the folk tale Reynard The Fox.

Then said the King, 'Now, by my crown, I will take such revenge as shall make that traitor tremble;' and sending for his counsellors, they decided that Reynard should be again summoned to court, and that Tibert the Cat should be the bearer of the message. 'It is your wisdom, Sir Tibert, I employ,' said the great King, 'and not your strength: many prevail with art, when violence returns with lost labour.'

So Tibert made ready, and set out with the King's letter to Malepardus, where he found the fox standing before his castle-gates; to whom Tibert said, 'Health to my fair cousin Reynard; the King, by me, summons you to the court, in which if you fail, there is nothing more assured unto you than a cruel and a sudden death.'

The fox answered, 'Welcome, dear cousin Tibert; I obey your command, and wish my Lord the King infinite days of happiness; only let me entreat you to rest with me to-night, and take such cheer as my simple house affordeth, and to-morrow, as early as you will, we will go towards the court, for I have no kinsman I trust so dearly as yourself.

From *The History of Reynard the Fox*

1 Find out about the Reynard stories and decide if you agree that the name Tybalt helps the audience to understand his character.

2 Think together to decide what you think about Tybalt's character and behaviour during these scenes:

- fighting on the street as the play opens;

- at the Capulet's party;

- looking for Romeo, to start another fight;

- fighting with Mercutio;

- fighting with Romeo;

- his relatives remember him; and

- Romeo remembers him.

3   Think together to say whether Tybalt's death, or
    Mercutio's death, seems more of a loss; and
    which has more influence on the remaining
    characters in the play.

4   Choose your relatives! Decide whether your
    group would prefer to be Montagues or
    Capulets, starting with thinking about Tybalt and Mercutio.

7 TALKING POINTS: LIGHT IN ACT 1

The following quotations include all the uses of the word 'light' in Act 1.

■   Think together to decide if 'light' is used literally or metaphorically.

■   Decide what these uses of 'light' tell us about each character, and the
    action of the play.

Montague
Away from the light steals home my heavy son,
And private in his chamber pens himself,
Shuts up his windows, locks fair daylight out

Romeo
O heavy lightness! serious vanity!

Capulet
Earth-treading stars that make dark heaven light

Romeo
Give me a torch: I am not for this ambling;
Being but heavy, I will bear the light.

Romeo, *on Cupid*
I am too sore enpierced with his shaft
To soar with his light feathers
A torch for me: let wantons light of heart
Tickle the senseless rushes with their heels

Mercutio
Up to the ears. Come, we burn daylight, ho!
    [. . .]
We waste our lights in vain, like lamps by day.

Capulet
More light, you knaves; and turn the tables up,
(To Tybalt) Be quiet, or — More light, more
        light!
For shame! I'll make you quiet.

8 TALKING POINTS: WORD USE IN *ROMEO AND JULIET*

1   Use an electronic version of the play to search for 'light' in Acts 2–5.

Decide how Shakespeare is using the word 'light'.

Think about the implications of 'light' as each character speaks.

Decide what ideas are associated with light and dark; light and heavy;
light hearted and unhappy; light meaning enlightened compared to
mysterious or unintelligent.

Think how these ideas add to our perception of the character speaking,
or what they are telling us about.

2   Use an electronic version of the play to search for other key words.

Use your search to say:

■   how Shakespeare depicts characters; and

■   how Shakespeare builds up word pictures of emotions, moods or
    feelings.

Key words (examples): light, day, sun, moon, dark, night, shadow, death,
life, love, hate, truth.

---

9 TALKING POINTS: CONTRASTS IN *ROMEO AND JULIET*

In *Romeo and Juliet*, Shakespeare uses direct and indirect contrasts between physical phenomena like 'light and dark', emotions like 'love and hate', and absolutes like 'truth and lies' to enrich the dialogue and portray a complex, difficult world.

- Decide which of the contrasts your group would like to examine.

- Using the play text, find examples of contrast in word use and action.

- Prepare a presentation to show your findings to the rest of the class. Your presentation should show how contrast is achieved and sustained, and the impact on characters and events.

- You can dramatise parts of the play; use a character to highlight ideas; use word cards; provide definitions and quotations; and put together an electronic presentation to structure how you will talk to the class.

- Keep a record of important acts, scenes and line numbers for reference later.

Examples of contrasts in *Romeo and Juliet*

a   Romantic love and true love –

spiritual, emotional, unrealistic, idealised **contrasted with** irrational, aggressive, fierce, enduring.

b   Fate and fortune –

The events of our lives are pre-determined, 'hanging in the stars' **contrasted with** our human ability to make choices depending on free will; ' I defy you, stars!'

More examples of contrasts

Light and dark	Passion and apathy
Day and night	Child and adult
Love and hate	Loyalty and disloyalty
Life and death	Religion and magic
Truth and lies	Murder and suicide
Good intentions, bad outcomes	Social life and privacy
Obedience and disobedience	Ruling class and servant class

Talking Points: *Richard III*

Introduction to
Richard III

Shakespeare does not follow a strict historical record of the Wars of the Roses. He is unconcerned with dates and never mentions them. He alters the sequence of events and the timing between events to make the play vibrant and to bring what is portrayed here as Richard's catalogue of crimes to life. This is of course only one side of the story, and there are many who would defend *Richard III*. This play deals with the death of Richard's brother Edward IV, and the confusion and intrigue that followed, culminating in the crowning of Richard and his death in almost the last battle in the long-drawn-out Wars of the Roses. Shakespeare dramatises in this play the fall of the House of York and the establishment of the Lancastrian Tudor monarchs.

For each scene of the play *context* is provided, which is largely based on the Shakespearian version of events. This is intended as brief support for the Talking Points. Students will need a copy of the play text. The aim is primarily to engage students with the text and ensure that they understand the characters, action, narrative and language of the play. Out of this may come an interest in the history; a Thinking Together activity to do with matching Shakespeare's version of events to the historical record is provided after the scene-by-scene Talking Points.

A NOTE ABOUT NAMES IN THE PLAY

In the play *Richard III*, there is every chance for confusion about who is who. There are four Edwards, two Richards, two Margarets, two Henrys, two Elizabeths, and two men called Hastings. Stanley is also called Derby, and George is also called Clarence. People are called by their titles, Christian names or surnames so that Richard may be called The Duke of Gloucester or just Gloucester, until he is Richard III. The Queen's brother is called Anthony Woodville. He is Earl Rivers, so is referred to as Rivers, but sometimes Richard calls him Woodville. All this adds a layer of difficulty for the student. Shakespeare himself found it complicated; in Act 2 Scene 1 line 69, three lords are addressed – Lord Rivers, Lord Woodville, and Lord Scales – though actually all these titles belonged to one character, Queen Elizabeth's brother Anthony Woodville.

For clarity the characters are referred to in the Talking
Points as follows:

- The main character is Richard.

- Edwards: the King as the play begins is Edward
  IV. His sons (Richard's nephews the 'Princes in
  the Tower') are Edward Prince of Wales (later
  Edward V) and Richard Duke of York. Crown Prince Edward who died at
  Tewkesbury in 1471 is referred to as Edward Tudor. The young son of
  George Duke of Clarence is Edward Plantagenet.

- Henry Earl of Richmond who arrives to give battle at Bosworth is Henry
  VII. The previous king, killed at Tewksbury, is Henry VI.

- King Edward IV's wife is Queen Elizabeth and their daughter is Princess
  Elizabeth.

- Stanley is referred to by many of the Players, though in the cast list he is
  called Derby. I have used both names e.g. Thomas Stanley (Earl of Derby).

- George Duke of Clarence is referred to as George or Clarence.

PREPARING FOR THE PLAY

Thinking Together activities

1 Mind map for *Richard III*

With a group, make a drawing, model or electronic image of each of the main
characters in the play. Arrange them on a poster (or board or screen) linking them
with lines annotated to show relationships at the start of the play. As the play
proceeds, move, alter or add further description to the characters or the linking
relationships, to show what is happening and why, and how this affects others.
Add feelings, prophesies and predictions as well as actual events, plans and
quotations.

Characters for your mind map

- King Edward IV.

- *Sons of King Edward IV*: Edward Prince of Wales and Richard Duke of York.

- *Brothers of King Edward*: George Duke of Clarence and Richard Duke
  of Gloucester.

- *Wife of King Edward*: Queen Elizabeth.

- *Daughter of King Edward:* Princess Elizabeth.
- *Brother of Queen Elizabeth:* Anthony Woodville Lord Rivers.
- *Sons of Queen Elizabeth:* Marquess of Dorset and Lord Grey.
- *Mother of King Edward and of George and Richard:* Duchess of York.
- *Daughter of Warwick The Kingmaker and widow of Edward Tudor:* Lady Anne.

- *Widow of King Henry VI and mother of Edward Tudor:* Queen Margaret.
- *Children of George Duke of Clarence:* Margaret and Edward Plantagenet.
- *Dukes and Lords:* Earl of Derby (also called Lord Stanley), Buckingham (who is Richard's friend), Norfolk, Hastings, Oxford (and others).
- *Keeper of the Tower of London:* Sir Robert Brackenbury.

2 Richard's claim to the throne of England

A summary of Richard's problem

You will need a family tree of:

a Edward III and his descendants.

b Edmund Langley Duke of York and his descendants (The House of York).

The contest for the crown arose because Edward III's son Richard II could have been succeeded by the descendents of his brother Lionel Duke of Clarence, third son of Edward III. Lionel's descendents in the House of York were eligible through the marriage of Anne Mortimer, Lionel's daughter, to Richard Earl of Cambridge, who was the son of the fifth son of Edward III. Instead, the succession went to the Lancastrian Henry IV, son of John of Gaunt, the fourth son of Edward III. These people were all related, so the battles between them were initially known as 'The Cousins' War' and later the Wars of the Roses, with the Lancastrians having a red rose for their symbol, and the Yorkists a white rose.

Discuss the family trees and the problem of succession.

Can you argue for the Yorkist cause? For the Lancastrian cause?

Try to make explicit your reasons for supporting either side.

Which side would your group join?

Richard III Talking Points scene by scene

Context

The Yorkist King Edward IV is back on the throne, having previously been deposed by the Tudor King Henry VI with the help of Richard Neville, Earl of Warwick ('The Kingmaker'). The symbol on the Yorkist flag is a sun. Edward, when young, secretly married Elizabeth Woodville, widow of Sir John Grey; she has a brother Anthony and two sons from her first marriage. Edward IV's younger brothers – George Duke of Clarence, and Richard – despise Elizabeth and fear her great influence on their brother the King. But King Edward IV has fallen ill. His sons, the young Prince of Wales Edward and his brother Richard Duke of York have a very close relationship with the Woodvilles. Richard fears that he will have little influence or power if either of them inherits the crown.

But the young princes are the legitimate heirs to the throne. Edward IV's brother George Duke of Clarence has been arrested and taken to the Tower of London. After the young princes, he is third in line to the throne and so he is a threat to them. Also, there have been rumours that Edward IV was not a legitimate son of his father Richard Plantagenet, and so his family line should not have the kingship. George Duke of Clarence does not know why he is imprisoned, but suspects that Edward IV's wife Queen Elizabeth has been plotting against him. Queen Elizabeth's sons from her previous marriage – the Marquess of Dorset and Lord Grey – are not of royal lineage and her Woodville family are regarded with great suspicion by the House of York family. Richard (who is currently the Duke of Gloucester) is Edward IV and George Duke of Clarence's younger brother, and so after the young princes and George, is fourth in line to the throne. Edward IV has a mistress – Mistress Shore – who is also the mistress of the rich and influential Lord Hastings. Lord Hastings is linked by marriage to the Tudors.

Richard is about thirty years old. Previously he has fought for his brother Edward IV in many battles, and been loyal to him. His soldiers fight with his sign, a boar,

on their armour. In Shakespeare's account, Richard is physically handicapped; he has a curved spine, a limp, and a 'withered' arm.

Richard grew up in turbulent times, his life influenced by the violent Wars of the Roses. His father Richard Plantagenet (1412–60) challenged the Lancastrian King Henry VI's right to the throne. After many battles both Richard's father and his brother, Edmund Earl of Rutland, were killed by Lancastrian forces led by Margaret of Anjou – Queen Margaret in the play. On 21 December 1460 Richard Plantagenet ('The Grand old Duke of York') marched out of Sandal Castle in Yorkshire, to be surrounded by Lancastrians 'like a fish in a net'. He and Edmund were killed at this battle, the battle of Wakefield. Their heads were impaled on the city walls at York, Richard's wearing a paper crown to further shame him.

Richard III: Talking Points Act 1 Scene 1

1 Richard finds peace time far too dull.

2 Richard has low self esteem.

3 Richard acts alone.

4 Richard uses a range of contrasting ideas to highlight the change from war to peace.

5 He has decided that he has the right to become king.

6 Richard's account for Brackenbury of his conversation with Clarence should make both of them wary of him.

7 Brackenbury is afraid of Richard.

8 Richard is unbelievably evil.

9 Richard must eliminate all who stand between him and the throne. To do so is cruel and profoundly wicked – not characteristics needed in a king.

10 Richard is highly devious and capable of carrying out deception.

11 Richard has no doubt at all that he can achieve his ambition.

12 Richard is enjoying himself.

13 His aim in intending to marry Anne is unclear at this point.

RICHARD III: ACT 1 SCENE 2

Context

Henry VI was King of England before Edward IV. A long and bitter set of wars took place – the Wars of the Roses – in which the crown was disputed between the House of York (symbol: red rose) and the House of Lancaster (symbol: white rose). The Tudor family were seen as usurpers of the crown by the Yorks. To 'usurp' means to illegally take the crown by force. Henry VI was married to Margaret, a french princess; they had one son, Edward Tudor. He was married to Anne Neville who was fourteen years old at the time. Anne was the younger daughter of the powerful and rich Richard Neville, the Earl of Warwick. Richard as a child lived in Warwick's household so he actually knew Anne well. She is a rich heiress and her father's name would win Richard many allies. In trying to regain the crown Henry VI's son Edward Tudor was killed in battle at Tewksbury by Richard.

Henry VI was captured and soon afterwards died in the Tower of London (perhaps killed by the York brothers). Anne Neville and Edward Tudor had been married for about five months. Richard was fighting for the crown – so that his brother Edward IV could be king.

Richard III: Talking Points Act 1 Scene 2

1 Anne has good reason to hate Richard.

2 Richard is frighteningly aggressive and determined, which is why he gets his own way. That sort of person often wins, though it does not seem to make them happy. It is difficult for others, who are more sensitive or thoughtful, to match such extreme behaviour.

3 The guards, who could ignore him or fight with him, give up too easily because of his air of authority.

4 Anne could not say more to express her loathing of Richard. But she is helpless and they both know it. Calling on heaven for help is a desperate and futile measure.

5 Richard has carefully thought in advance what he will say to Anne in this encounter.

6 Richard's words 'your bedchamber' are outrageous in this context.

7 Richard is controlling and cruel. He aims to convince Anne that she somehow caused her husband's death; this is ridiculous, but once Richard has insisted on the idea, she is weakened by his assertiveness.

8 Anne takes a real risk when she spits at Richard. It is astonishing that he does not take physical action at this point.

9 Anne cannot kill Richard. Few people can turn themselves into killers – the forces against killing others are too strong. Richard knows this.

10 We cannot tell why Anne abruptly abandons cursing and hating Richard and takes his ring. Maybe her upbringing, as part of a political world, over-rides her personal feelings. She has been raised to marry a king and maybe she sees Richard as her next best chance. Maybe she is just heartlessly ambitious. Maybe she is really persuaded by him. Maybe she suddenly sees herself as a kind of saviour of Richard.

11 Richard despises Anne.

12 Richard can hardly believe that he has so easily changed Anne's mind.

13 Richard regrets the death of Edward Tudor.

14 Richard is impressed by his own devilry and power.

RICHARD III: ACT 1 SCENE 3

Context

Queen Elizabeth knows her husband Edward IV is dangerously ill. She is afraid he will die. Her fear is for herself, because his heir, her son Edward aged twelve is too young to reign, and she knows that there will be chaos until the succession is organised. She thinks that she will be marginalised and that her sons' lives will be in danger. She is aware that Richard is her enemy. Her brother and sons cannot reassure her. She is older than Edward, a commoner, and he defied his family to marry her. Richard cannot forgive her for her influence over Edward, and for the ambitious way that she has gained positions of power for members of her family.

Historically Queen Margaret died before the action of the play begins, but is included by Shakespeare to present the background to Richard's villainy and to emphasise his part in the transfer of power to the House of York from the Tudors. She adds weight to the chorus of voices denouncing Richard as a demon.

Richard III: Talking Points Act 1 Scene 3

1 Elizabeth knows that to insist on friendship between her relatives and Richard is futile.

2 Richard exaggerates the enmity between the Woodvilles and himself so that he can blame them for Clarence's death. They have no idea what he is doing.

3 Richard takes some risk in being so rude and forthright, because after all, Elizabeth is queen.

4 Richard is particularly scathing to Rivers because the Woodvilles are 'commoners' whereas he can trace his lineage back to kings.

5 Richard fought for Edward in the war. This gives him some right to position himself as more important than Elizabeth's family who were on the Lancastrian side.

6 Queen Margaret is a much stronger opponent for Richard than either Elizabeth or Anne – because she has nothing left to lose.

7 Richard is a little afraid of Margaret, and tricks her into cursing herself because of his fear of her power.

8 Queen Margaret is frantically jealous of Elizabeth.

9 Margaret is seen as 'lunatic' although actually, her understanding of Richard is more perceptive and realistic than that of the others present.

10 Richard's hypocrisy is transparent but the Woodvilles are simple enough to find it believable.

11 Richard in a soliloquy explains his new strategy. The other people he has encountered in the play so far have had no impact on his thinking.

12 Richard's instructions to the murderers are particularly evil.

13 Richard is more friendly and honest with the murderers than he has been with anyone else – they are his sort of people.

RICHARD III: ACT 1 SCENE 4

Context

George Duke of Clarence fought in battles in France and England for his brother Edward IV to be king. He has remained loyal to Edward despite the Woodville marriage. He may see his younger brother Richard as his friend and ally. They have previously been in dispute over the inheritance of money belonging to their wives Isabelle and Anne Neville. He regrets the acts of aggression he carried out in war. He is a widower; he blamed his wife Isabelle's death on a servant and had her put to death; but Isabelle's death was probably because of tuberculosis. His two surviving children are Margaret and Edward Plantagenet.

The Tower of London is a prison and a symbol of power. It was built as a fortress for William the Conqueror following the Norman invasion of 1066. There have been prisoners at the Tower almost since it was built. For over 900 years traitors, kings, queens, lords, ladies and ordinary people have been imprisoned here. In addition it offered a place of safety, where important people could be guarded, and the living quarters for the wealthy were well furnished and comfortable.

Richard III: Talking Points Act 1 Scene 4

1 Clarence's dream is a nightmare. Dreams are a mix of imagination and real things we have in our minds. It appears that Clarence has a good idea what is about to happen, and why.

2 A dream that continues after death is a really strange idea.

3 Clarence regrets putting wealth and power before human feeling.

4 Clarence regrets his part as a soldier in the wars that made his brother king.

5 Brackenbury and the Keeper know what is going to happen. They mindlessly obey the order written in the Warrant. This is how soldiers are trained to behave.

6 There are two murderers because either one of them would not have gone through with it alone.

7 The murderers find it hard to take action until they focus their thinking on the reward they will receive.

8 What Richard told them about talking to Clarence was true.

9 The Second Murderer is a much nastier person than the First Murderer because he is weak willed and easily bribed.

10 In films, the 'baddies' talk to their victims and usually this gives the victim time to find a way out, or somehow escape death. That is not the point of the talk that the murderers have with Clarence.

11 Clarence is aware that he has committed murder himself, but sees it as forgivable in the context of war.

12 The Second Murderer acts too late to save Clarence because he really wants the money.

13 We are left feeling angry with the Second Murderer because he was the only person with one chance to save Clarence, and he did not act.

RICHARD III: ACT 2 SCENE 1

Context

Edward IV knows that he is terminally ill and calls his relatives to him. He thinks that he can make them behave as he wishes even after he is dead. His aim is to ensure that the kingdom remains peaceful while his sons are too young to reign. He is trying to ensure that his 'line' continues to rule England. Also, the country has been through years of war and he knows that peace is crucial for prosperity. He has no idea of Richard's treachery, but he knows that his own family really despise his wife Queen Elizabeth and her family the Woodvilles.

Richard III: Talking Points Act 2 Scene 1

1 Hastings, Rivers, Queen Elizabeth, Dorset, and Buckingham, are all insincere and just saying what the King wants to hear so that they appear compliant.

2 Elizabeth resents being included in the King's list of people who have been behaving badly.

3 Everything is going well until Richard arrives.

4 Richard uses his knowledge of Clarence's death to ensure that enmity continues.

5 Richard is quite happy to make his dying brother Edward feel dreadfully guilty.

6 The King and Queen blame one another for Clarence's death.

7 The shocking news makes each of those present aware that their own death may be next – they deeply distrust one another.

8 Richard's plan is working well so far.

RICHARD III: ACT 2 SCENE 2

Context

The Duchess of York (Cecily Neville) was married to
Richard Plantagenet (1412–60); she is the mother of
King Edward IV, George Duke of Clarence, and Richard. She also had a fourth
son, Edmund (Rutland), who was killed aged seventeen by the Lancastrian Lord
Clifford at the battle of Wakefield. She has just heard that her son Clarence has
been executed in the Tower of London. This could not have happened without
a royal warrant. Clarence's attitude to the Woodvilles had irritated Edward IV and
he had been accused of treason. But she does not know exactly what happened
to him or who is responsible. She suspects her daughter-in-law Queen Elizabeth's
family. However she is also fearfully aware of her son Richard's capacity to lie,
murder and commit atrocious crimes to get what he wants.

Richard III: Talking Points Act 2 Scene 2

1 You can see where Richard learnt to tell lies – his mother lies to her
grandchildren about their father's death.

2 It is ridiculous to say that sorrow for those who have died is 'lost'. Sorrow
is a natural and appropriate response to death.

3 The Duchess is right; when people are evil their parents are actually
responsible for their actions.

4 The Duchess pities herself for losing a son. She does not really regret the
loss of Edward IV.

5 The Queen and the Duchess start a competition: who is the most sorry for
themselves. They are both selfish.

6 They hate one another.

7 The children are a nuisance and should be sent out of the room.

8 You cannot measure grief and decide who has most.

9 Dorset tries to say that they should be grateful for Edward's life, but no one
is listening.

10 Richard has no respect for his mother, but you can see why.

11 The Duchess of York thinks she should still be parenting Richard and trying to make him behave better. Quite rightly, he resents this.

12 Buckingham shows disloyalty to the Queen by being rude about her family.

13 Richard needs Buckingham as part of his plot, not as a friend.

RICHARD III: ACT 2 SCENES 3 AND 4

Context

The long history of war has left the people of England troubled. They know that the death of the King will destabilise the fragile peace. They also know that the land cannot be securely governed by a child king. The long drawn out Wars of the Roses (*note*: not known as such in Shakespeare's time) have made the people wary of change, and wary of taking sides; their only safe course is to support whoever wins the battle, or is actually crowned. They also know that the Woodville family have assumed power under Queen Elizabeth, and they resent this.

Richard Duke of York (aged ten) is with his mother Queen Elizabeth and his grandmother The Duchess of York, in London; they await the arrival of Edward V. He is being escorted by the Woodvilles from Ludlow to London, for his coronation. On the way, Richard catches up with them at Stony Stratford and arrests the Woodvilles, claiming that they intended to harm him and others. Richard in effect captures Edward V, while appearing to be there to protect him. He arrests the Woodville uncles, dismisses Edward's retinue of soldiers, and threatens all of Edward V's close supporters and household with death if they do not leave. With his own troops in place, he then escorts the understandably upset Edward to London; the boy is a prisoner from the moment Richard sees him.

'Sanctuary' in this context means a sacred place, such as a church, in which fugitives can remain to take shelter from the law or from political opponents. People in sanctuary are safe from arrest. Queen Elizabeth had already lived in sanctuary while Henry IV was on the throne; she lived in great luxury with a large household to look after her and her children.

Richard III: Talking Points Act 2 Scene 3 and 4

1 Scene 2 creates an air of impending trouble.

2 The play would do well without these two scenes; we learn nothing from them.

3 Scene 2 is about a king's fitness to rule.

4 People are right that a child should not be allowed to be king.

5 People are unduly pessimistic about everything.

6 The Duke of York is arrogant and unpleasant.

7 Queen Elizabeth over-reacts to the news from the north.

8 Sanctuary cannot be found in a kingdom where Richard is organising everything.

RICHARD III: ACT 3 SCENE 1

Context

With George Duke of Clarence dead, Richard is now third in line to the throne after the young princes. Edward Prince of Wales (aged twelve) has arrived in London. During the journey Richard has captured the boy's uncles – the Woodvilles – and ordered their imprisonment in his castle at Pomfret in Yorkshire. Richard has also persuaded Buckingham to agree with his idea of claiming the throne instead of young Edward. Partly because he despises the Woodvilles (the Prince of Wales' mother Elizabeth is a Woodville) Buckingham goes along with this.

Richard III: Talking Points Act 3 Scene 1

1 Edward Duke of York trusts Richard.

2 Richard is fond of Edward.

3 Buckingham argues that the Duke of York cannot be in sanctuary. His reasons are sound.

4 Buckingham knows that Richard wishes to kill the princes.

5 Meeting with Edward has not made Richard change his mind about murdering him; this shows him to be almost inhuman.

6 The young Duke of York is mouthy and rude.

7 The Duke of York really annoys both Richard and his older brother Edward.

8 They could refuse to go to the Tower if they tried harder.

9 Buckingham says things that Richard has convinced him to say.

10 Buckingham and Catesby are genuinely trying to find out whether Hastings and Stanley will side with them or with the Woodvilles.

11 Richard's comment about Hastings, 'Chop off his head!' seems like a joke to Buckingham, but Richard means it.

RICHARD III: ACT 3 SCENE 2

Context

Lord Stanley (Earl of Derby) and Lord Hastings are very powerful landowners and noblemen in the service of the court. Whoever is king needs their loyalty. They can raise large armies if they so wish. Sir William Catesby is one of Richard's close allies, a trained lawyer, Chancellor of the Exchequer and Speaker of the House of Commons. They have all been afraid of the growing power of the Queen's relatives and are glad that Richard is sorting out this problem. Hastings was previously imprisoned in the tower because of the Queen's fear of his connection to the Tudors through his wife, but at that time was released.

Richard III: Talking Points Act 3 Scene 2

1 Lord Stanley mistrusts Richard.

2 Hastings is right to think that flight is a way to provoke attack.

3 Catesby's news – that Richard is expecting to be king – horrifies Hastings because he knows Richard is corrupt, and also because he wants the young Edward to be king so that he can control him.

4 Richard has not just imprisoned the Woodvilles, but ordered their execution although actually they have done nothing wrong.

5 Hastings does not think clearly or he would be more careful what he says to Catesby.

6 Catesby knows of Richard's plan to kill Hastings and this makes him devious and cruel.

7 Hastings making fun of Derby (Stanley) for being afraid of Richard tells us a lot about what sort of person he is.

8 Buckingham believes that Hastings is merely going to be imprisoned.

RICHARD III: ACT 3 SCENE 3

Context

Pomfret (Pontefract) is a castle in south Yorkshire belonging to Richard. King Richard II was murdered at this castle in 1400. Anthony Woodville (Earl Rivers), Lord Grey (Queen Elizabeth's grown up son) and Sir Thomas Vaughn know that they are there to be killed and that Richard has put them there. Grey and Rivers were at the battle of Tewksbury where Richard stabbed the Tudor Crown Prince Edward to death. They have been closely involved with bringing up the young King Edward V (as yet uncrowned); he is fond of them and their influence is very strong. Richard feared that his position as Protector would be completely undermined if they had reached London. He fears the loss of power; he sees himself as having a right to govern. Richard insists that the Woodvilles are traitors and sets out to convince others that they tried to murder himself and Buckingham.

Richard III: Talking Points Act 3 Scene 3

1 The prisoners try to convince their jailers that they too are at risk as a last-ditch attempt to avoid death.

2 The prisoners are afraid and angry and sorry for themselves.

3 They believe that their death is caused by Margaret's curse.

4 The guards are implacable, which is how they should be.

RICHARD III: ACT 3 SCENE 4

Context

The lords of the realm were responsible for deciding on
the day and time of a new king's coronation. In this case
they meet at Crosby House (Richard's house in Bishopsgate) to discuss the
coronation of the uncrowned Edward V. Edward himself is lodged for the night
at the Bishop of London's palace, nearby. In this scene Richard accuses Queen
Elizabeth of witchcraft. He also implicates Mistress Shore, King Edward IV's
mistress. She had previously had a relationship with Hastings and this fact is common
knowledge at court. Despite his strongly moral stance, Richard is believed to have
at least two 'natural' children (that is, not born to his wife).

Richard III: Talking Points Act 3 Scene 4

1 Buckingham's assertion – 'for our hearts, he knows no more of mine than I
   of yours, or I of his' – is true.

2 The strawberries are irrelevant.

3 Hastings is totally fooled by Richard.

4 Richard's shocking attack on Hastings comes out of the blue to most people
   present.

5 Too late, Hastings realises what Richard plans.

6 Hastings would have supported Richard in his bid for kingship, if he had
   been given chance to think things through.

RICHARD III: ACT 3 SCENE 5

Context

Richard has killed his brother Clarence and three key members of the Woodville family, imprisoned the young princes in the tower, and sent Hastings to be hastily executed without trial, as part of his plan to reign as king. He now needs allies. He is aware that if the princes survive to adulthood, his rather tenuous claim to the throne will be vigorously disputed. He must convince everyone of various ill-prepared claims, such as that since their mother Elizabeth was previously married and widowed, the boys, though Edward's sons, are not truly 'legitimate' and therefore cannot be in line for the throne. He generates alternative rumours such as that Edward IV was not legitimate. In order to claim the throne, Richard must maintain that he is entitled to it; he has to have a right to it, and every other candidate must be seen as unfit to rule.

Richard III: Talking Points Act 3 Scene 5

1 Buckingham convinces Richard that he will act a part to support him.

2 Buckingham trusts Richard.

3 Buckingham is mortally afraid of Richard because he knows how ruthless he is.

4 Richard is a bully who cannot expect to have loyal allies; people do what he wants out of fear not friendship.

5 Richard is getting increasingly reckless.

6 Buckingham really believes that Hastings was a traitor.

7 The Lord Mayor is unbelievably gullible – or simply a coward.

8 The idea that Edward IV was not his father's son is ridiculous.

9 Buckingham is a puppet.

10 Richard does not confide his plans for the princes to anyone, because he does not trust anyone.

RICHARD III: ACT 3 SCENE 6 AND 7

Context

Richard's plan has flaws; even the scrivener (scribe) who writes of the execution of Hastings can see that things are happening in the wrong order. At this time, no king has been crowned, and everyone is waiting to see who to side with. There is little trust between people, and unscrupulous bullies like Richard are able to make things go their way. While preparations are made for the coronation, the boy king Edward V and his younger brother are taken to the Tower. This is not unusual; since the fourteenth century the coronation procession had set out from the Tower to Westminster Abbey. The children of George, Duke of Clarence are also something of a threat – they also have a claim to the throne. Richard has to orchestrate many different plots and he has no one to confide in. He is relying on the story that Edward IV when young underwent a marriage ceremony with a sister of the French King; if true this means that his marriage with Elizabeth Woodville was 'bigamy' – and their son Edward Prince of Wales cannot rule.

Richard III: Talking Points Act 3 Scene 6 and 7

1 Buckingham really does his best to make Richard the new king.

2 The citizens do not like Richard and do not want him to be king.

3 Buckingham is doing all this so that he can have money and lands when Richard is king.

4 Richard and Buckingham have rehearsed this scene.

5 Buckingham describes Elizabeth Woodville in extremely insulting terms.

6 Catesby is not part of Richard's plot.

7 What Buckingham says about Edward IV is true.

8 Richard's reluctance is all still part of his plan – but it is hard to act this way and be believable.

9 Buckingham is very trusting; he should know better.

RICHARD III: ACT 4 SCENE 1

Context

The Marquess of Dorset is Queen Elizabeth's son from her first marriage. He was not killed with the other Woodvilles at Pomfret. Stanley, Earl of Derby sends Dorset as an envoy to Henry Tudor, Earl Richmond who lives in Brittany. Henry Tudor is son of Margaret Beaufort and Edmund Tudor Earl of Richmond, themselves descendants of the Lancastrian John of Gaunt. This gives Henry Tudor a valid claim to the throne. After the death of Edmund Tudor, Margaret married Thomas Stanley (Earl of Derby) and their son, later captured and held hostage by Richard, is called George.

Richard III: Talking Points Act 4 Scene 1

1 Brackenbury is still following orders mindlessly, as he did when the murderers came to visit Clarence.

2 Dorset is a coward.

3 Thomas Stanley, Earl of Derby is beginning to suspect Richard of treason – but is still acting for him, mainly out of fear.

4 Queen Elizabeth is powerless to protect her sons.

5 Anne is just pretending she does not want to marry Richard.

RICHARD III: ACT 4 SCENES 2 AND 3

Context

Richard III is crowned, and married to Anne Neville. He is king but is insecure; he cannot forget that the two princes, his brother's sons, could rightfully claim the throne. They are Edward, aged twelve and Richard, aged ten. He plans to imprison Clarence's son and arrange a hasty marriage for Clarence's daughter, so that they are no longer a threat. He also plans to have Anne killed so that he can marry Princess Elizabeth; she is his niece and is about 20 years younger than he is. As king he is very isolated and fearful. He has achieved what he set out to by violence and cunning. He expects others to act the same way and so is aware that he is in an extremely dangerous position. Buckingham has been loyal and done everything possible to support Richard's claim to the throne, and he now expects to be rewarded as Richard promised.

Richard III: Talking Points Act 4 Scenes 2 and 3

1 Richard has changed now he is king. He is no longer witty and well organised.

2 Richard asks too much of Buckingham.

3 The plan to kill both princes is hasty and reckless – but no more so than the plans to kill Clarence or Hastings.

4 Buckingham has finally come to a point where he shows some morality.

5 Buckingham's honest shock tips Richard into murderous rage.

6 For Richard to trust a page is really stupid.

7 Richard's plan to kill his two young nephews and his wife proves he is a monster.

8 Initially Richard plans to ask Tyrrel to murder Buckingham.

9 We do not know what Buckingham intended to say to Richard about the plan to kill the princes. He might have agreed.

10 Buckingham has lost his wits and chooses completely the wrong time to remind Richard about the promise of land and money.

11 Tyrrel's account of the death of the princes is romantic but still horrifying.

12 The news of rebellion against Richard, led by Buckingham, is not surprising.

13 Richard is relieved when the opposition becomes apparent. He is ready to fight.

14 After the death of the princes, Richard is constantly surprised by events. He is now in defence rather than on the attack.

RICHARD III: ACT 4 SCENE 4

Context

Queen Margaret is very old – over eighty. Richard, with his brother Clarence, killed her husband Henry VI (Harry) and her son Edward Tudor.

The Duchess of York is Richard III's mother. Richard killed her second son, his brother Clarence. Her husband and her young son Edmund were killed by Margaret's husband and son.

Queen Elizabeth (Woodville) was married to The Duchess of York's eldest son Edward. Richard killed her brother, her sons from a previous marriage, and her two young sons, the princes in the Tower. She is so afraid of him that she remains in sanctuary. He plans to marry her young daughter.

Thomas Stanley Earl of Derby has a son, George Stanley, and his wife is mother of the Tudor Henry, Earl of Richmond. Richard distrusts Derby but has so few friends that he continues to rely on him.

Richmond collects an army to march against Buckingham and then against Henry, Earl of Richmond. Some of Richard's allies defect to the opposition. Henry, Earl of Richmond, the Tudor (Lancastrian) heir to the throne, makes one attempt to land in Dorset and is beaten back by bad weather; he sails around the coast to Wales and lands successfully there. He has loyal allies in Wales.

Richard marches towards Salisbury, on his way to Leicester, to join his troops from the north.

Richard III: Talking Points Act 4 Scene 4

1 The women in this scene are indistinguishable.

2 They have a right to complain.

3 They should stop whingeing and just leave the country or take sanctuary.

4 They list Richard's crimes; they do not console one another.

5 Richard is afraid of all three of them together.

6 He tries, but cannot ignore the Duchess of York's curse.

7 Richard lies almost by habit, for example denying he killed the princes.

8 He uses his previous argument – that he
   committed murders for the love of a woman –
   this time, Elizabeth – but his insincerity is
   completely obvious this time.

9 Richard is unbelievably patient with Queen
   Elizabeth. He has lost his ruthlessness.

10 Queen Elizabeth does not really believe his arguments, she just pretends.

11 Richard killed Queen Elizabeth's brothers and her young sons. She is able
   to forget this because she is so keen to be mother of the next queen.

12 Richard really thinks that marrying Princess Elizabeth will solve everything.

13 Richard is in a muddle and cannot think clearly how to organise his troops.
   The encounter with the women has bothered him.

14 Richard's mistakes and short temper make Catesby and Derby (Stanley)
   wary of him.

15 Taking Derby's son as hostage is not going to make Derby feel more
   loyal.

RICHARD III: ACT 4 SCENE 5

Context

Thomas Earl of Derby (Lord Stanley) is now well aware of Richard's crimes and
has no desire to side with him in war. However he knows that his life is at risk if
he defects. Worse, Richard has his young son George imprisoned as hostage. Lord
Stanley is married to Margaret, who is the Tudor Earl of Richmond's mother; this
is her second marriage. It means that he is Henry Tudor, Earl of Richmond's step
father. George Stanley, his son, is Richmond's step brother.

Richard III: Act 4 Scene 5 Talking Points

1 Derby is in a dangerous position, but keeps a cool head.

2 Derby has been Richard's enemy all along.

3 The letter could easily fall into the wrong hands.

4 Derby is brave.

5 Derby is a coward who can see that Richard is outnumbered – and he
   wants to be with the winning side.

RICHARD III: ACT 5 SCENE 1

Context

All Souls' Day, usually celebrated on 2 November, is the day in the Christian calendar when prayer for the souls of the dead enables their passage into heaven. It would also have been the thirteenth birthday of Edward V. Richard, hearing of Buckingham's treachery to his cause, referred to him as 'the most untrue creature living' and offered a reward of £1,000 for his capture. Buckingham's army of troops were thrown into disorder by torrential rain and flooding of the River Severn, and many of them left to return home. Buckingham sought refuge near Shrewsbury with a former family servant Ralph Banaster. Banaster betrayed him to the Sherriff of Shropshire who sent troops to capture him. Buckingham was not allowed to see Richard to ask forgiveness, but instead taken immediately to Salisbury and beheaded.

Richard III: Act 5 Scene 1 Talking Points

1 Buckingham feels real shame for his actions.

2 Buckingham had no thought of personal ambition, but acted entirely to support his hero Richard.

3 Buckingham should not have raised an army, but kept a low profile till things were sorted out.

4 Buckingham deserves to die as a traitor to King Edward IV, King Edward V, and King Richard.

RICHARD III: ACT 5 SCENES 2 AND 3

Context

Realising that Richard's subjects and countrymen were turning against him, and with the encouragement of the English lords, Henry Earl of Richmond sailed from Harfleur on the French coast with a small army. He was funded by Philip of France who wanted England to be unsettled in order to distract attention from his own plan to seize the land of Brittany. He arrived at Poole on the Dorset coast with only fifteen ships. The weather prevented his landing, which was probably fortunate because it is likely that he would have been captured. Instead, after failing to land in Dorset, Henry collected support and landed safely in at Mill Bay on the north side of Milford Haven. He gathered further support in Wales, marching north to Aberystwyth while his allies marched and collected support further south in Wales; these armies met up at Welshpool, crossed the English border, and marched together towards Leicester.

It is said that on 20 August 1485 when Richmond's small army reached Tamworth, they were dismayed to find that he was no longer with them. Riding at the rear of the troops, 'musing', he had inattentively taken a wrong direction and had no idea where he was. When it grew dark he found lodgings as 'an unimportant stranger' and only rejoined his army on 21 August – much to their relief.

Richard was at Nottingham Castle when he heard of the invasion. Richard perhaps thought it unnecessary to make great preparations to halt the march of a small army under an inexperienced commander. But once he realised that he would have to defend his crown, he sent for reinforcements from Northumberland and York.

Secretly, Richmond and his allies were in touch with Stanley Earl of Derby throughout the preparations for battle.

The opposing armies met just north of Market Bosworth in Leicestershire. On the night of 21 August 1485, both sets of soldiers set up camp. A contemporary journal, the Croyland Chronicle, reports that Richard slept badly before the battle and awoke with his face 'more livid and ghastly than usual'.

On the morning of the battle, Richmond commanded about 5,000 men. Richard commanded 20,000; but 4,000 of these were Stanley's men. Stanley had no intention of supporting Richard unless something disastrous happened to Richmond. In addition Northumberland's men did not engage in battle.

Richard III: Act 5 Scenes 2 and 3 Talking Points

1 Richmond's army feel that they have right on their side.

2 They are convinced that some of Richard's army may defect.

3 Richard is enjoying the activity of preparing for battle.

4 Both leaders make effective preparations for their armies.

5 Once night falls, Richard begins to feel afraid.

6 Richmond is more hopeful than certain that he can defeat Richard.

7 The ghosts remind us of the extent of Richard's crimes.

8 Richard wakes thinking he is in battle.

9 He finally faces the cruelty and barbarity of the killings he ordered.

10 Anyone who has committed so many murders is never going to stop.

11 Richard hates himself as much as others hate him.

12 Those who commit murder have little regard for life – including their own life.

13 He is sorry for himself.

14 Richard realises that there are 5,000 men outside his tent who want to kill him. It is this that troubles his sleep, not his past actions.

15 If you cannot sleep, it's a good idea to do something active.

16 Listeners never hear good of themselves, so he is not going to find comfort or courage by overhearing what his soldiers say.

17 Both leaders give speeches, which gives their soldiers courage.

18 Richmond is prepared to die as long as Richard does too.

19 Richard wastes preparation time fretting about the past.

20 The idea of battle invigorates Richard; he thinks it is what Kings do.

21 The note found by Norfolk is incomprehensible.

22 Richard motivates his troops by reminding them that the troops they face are 'foreigners'. He mentions their wives to give them a reason to show no mercy.

23 His speech is desperate. He depicts the enemy as weak and cowardly.

24 Richard does despair, as the ghosts told him to, and it is this that undermines his strength in battle.

25 The defection of Stanley is the last straw for Richard. He now knows he is doomed.

RICHARD III: ACT 5 SCENES 4 AND 5

Context

The Battle of Bosworth Field lasted about three hours.

The Battle of Bosworth was fought just south of Market
Harborough (Grid Reference SP394986). It was almost the last battle of the Wars
of the Roses, fought to decide whether Richard III or Henry VII would be king.
It was fought on 22 August 1485. The site of the battle has been disputed;
information is available at the battlefield visitor centre and web site.

Richard divided his army into three groups (or 'battles') commanded by the Duke
of Norfolk, Northumberland, and himself. Henry kept his force together under
the command of the Earl of Oxford.

Norfolk's men struggled against Oxford's. Northumberland's men held back, as
did Stanley's, leaving Richard's army weakened. Seeing his troops hampered by
mud and failing to defeat the enemy, Richard took a desperate direct charge of
mounted men across the field to try to kill Henry, who, inexperienced in battle,
had remained at the back of the field and left the fighting to Oxford. Richard
had taken part in many battles before, but this was still a fearless and bold move.
So that his soldiers could identify him, he was wearing his crown. Richard got
close enough to Henry to kill his standard bearer. But Henry's bodyguards closed
in and moved him to the rear of the battlefield where he was safe.

Stanley, seeing that Richard was struggling, then joined the battle, his men
surrounding Richard. Richard's banner man was killed. Richard's horse became
stuck in the deep mud of the marsh; he continued fighting on foot. Others offered
him their horses so that he could escape but he refused. The Croyland Chronicle
(1485) reports: 'King Richard received many mortal wounds and like a spirited
and most courageous prince, fell in battle on the field and not in flight.' He must
have been aware that defeat meant death anyway. He was killed on the field. With
Richard dead, the battle was abandoned. Richard's crown, a circlet, was found
(reportedly in a hawthorn bush) by Lord Stanley, who presented it to Henry Tudor.
Richard's body was taken naked, with a rope round his neck, across a horse to
Leicester for exhibition – to prove to the people that he was dead – and then for
a hasty burial in an unmarked grave. Recently archaeologists have discovered
Richard III's skeleton at Greyfriars Abbey in Leicester.

The battle was therefore won by the Lancastrian Richmond, Henry Tudor who
became Henry VII. This ended the Plantagenet or Yorkist reign. Henry VII later

married Princess Elizabeth, daughter of Edward IV; this meant that the houses of York and Lancaster were united in a way that ensured peace and prosperity for England. The Tudor Rose symbolises this, with its depiction of a double rose, white over red.

Richard III: Talking Points Act 5 Scenes 4 and 5

1 This battle is entirely about who will be king.

2 Richard fights ferociously.

3 Richard's soldiers really believe in him.

4 Richard was betrayed by the powerful Dukes Stanley and Northumberland.

5 Seeing his foot soldiers falling, Richard makes a desperate attempt to kill Henry.

6 Richard could have escaped.

7 Once Richard is killed, the battle becomes pointless, and it ends.

8 Henry, Earl of Richmond takes the crown as King Henry VII.

9 Henry VII usurped the crown.

10 His first thought is for George Stanley, his step brother, showing his humanity.

11 Richmond has a plan to ensure peace and prosperity.

12 Richmond is portrayed as almost saintly to contrast the Tudor monarchs with the Plantagents.

13 We feel no regret for Richard's death.

More Talking Points and Thinking Together for *Richard III*

1 *RICHARD III*: REASONING

Reasoning aloud with others can help to generate new understanding. It can be inspiring and interesting. It can also be very frustrating to try to explain what you think to others who do not want to listen, or who are instantly dismissive. A good discussion is the aim; in this section exploratory talk is used to support rational, courteous discussion, which helps everyone to move on in their thinking. Reasoning is crucial and can be based on *evidence* or *opinion*.

Reasoning to do with *evidence* draws on the following things: knowledge, particular sources of information, direct reference to texts, or on data. You can refer directly to Shakespeare's words, to a commentary about the play, to historical sources or to literary criticism and reviews.

Reasoning to do with *opinion* draws on: personal ideas, faith, beliefs, impressions or own understanding. You can offer your own analysis, evaluation, synthesis of ideas, thoughts or feelings.

Shakespeare's plays have been under discussion for over 400 years now. They are a resource for all of us. Fresh thinking about the plays is important; they were written for performance, not just for scholars and writers. The plays were written for people to see, hear, look at and enjoy in their own way. Reasoning about the play with others can help you to sort out what you think about Richard III.

In discussion with your group, be prepared to offer your reasons for what you think. Listen attentively. Can you be persuaded or influenced to change your mind? What use is it to consider a range of points of view, or different opinions? What convincing reasons do others give; what reasons stimulate further discussion? If your group disagrees, is it possible to use the play as a resource to help resolve things, or is other information needed?

Talk about these ideas; do you agree or disagree with them; what are your reasons? Compare your reasons to the points of view offered by others.

1 *Richard III* is not Shakespeare's best play.

2 The play is historically inaccurate. It is a tragedy, not a history.

3 The play was written to please the Tudor Queen, Elizabeth I.

4 None of the titled characters is really believable, but the 'common' people are.

5 Shakespeare grew to admire Richard III as he wrote the play.

6 Richard III is a villain but at first we think he is funny and clever.

7 Shakespeare uses Richard to investigate the nature of evil and power.

8 Richard's victims are all at some level partially responsible for the situations that they find themselves in.

9 The play is confusing because of all the similar names of characters.

10 You have to know some history to make sense of the play.

11 Before he kills the princes, Richard is in control. Afterwards, he is jittery and confused. A psychological change takes place at the end of Act 4 Scene 3. Richard never recovers his vision and drive. He has even appalled himself.

12 The battle is too brief and could be better described. It has to be acted for the power of it to become clear.

13 Shakespeare never mentions dates and has no interest in them.

More points to discuss and decide, giving your reasons:

14 Richard's (or, Shakespeare's) view of women generally is that they are simple, manipulative, immoral, jealous, interfering gossips. The women characters are inadequate. Shakespeare had not learned how to write good women's roles.

15 Shakespeare wrote this play when quite young. He had little experience of the death of a child, father or brother, and so his writing about these harrowing things is stylised and formulaic.

16 All the ill wishes contained in Anne's curse
(Act 2 Scene 1, 14–28) eventually happen to
Richard, either in the play, or in his real life.
Margaret's predictions (Act 1 Scene 3) all turn
into events that happen during the play. The
point about the predictions in the play is that
no one ever takes note of them, but individuals
remember them when they have come true –
or when it's too late.

17 Clarence's dream (Act 1 Scene 4) shows him trying to make sense of
events and feelings by relating a mixture of memory, imagination, and the
influence of 'conscience'. Analysis of the dream gives insight into Clarence's
real character, and the way he wants the keeper to see him, which are
different things.

18 In the fifteenth century blasphemy and anti-Christian thinking were illegal
and severely punished. There are many churchmen in the play; an
archbishop in Act 2 Scene 4, Cardinal Bouchier in Act 3 Scene 1, The
bishop of Ely in Act 3 Scene 4, two 'reverend fathers' in Act 3 Scene 7.
Many scenes require a religious presence, such as the funeral procession,
the coronation, taking sanctuary, and the executions. Richard fools no-one
with his display of religious belief. Richard is religious – or Richard is
sanctimonious.

19 Richard is called many disparaging names by various characters in the play;
find some effective insults and decide together what particular image of him
is built up by the vocabulary used.

20 Think together to decide if you agree that The Earl of Derby (Lord Stanley)
is an enigmatic character. Create and write 'thought bubbles' your group
would suggest for his appearance in these scenes – whether he actually
speaks or not. *(See Act 1 Scene 3; Act 2 Scene 2 (he is present as Richard's
supporter, but does not speak); Act 3 Scene 2; Act 3 Scene 4; Act 5 Scene 1;
then his actions in the battle scenes).*

21 The play's characters are concerned with the influence that conscience
can have on action. Think together to find out what each of your group
understands by the word 'conscience' and come to a working definition.
Decide if Clarence, Queen Margaret or Richard live by their conscience.

2 *RICHARD III*: THINKING TOGETHER

Richard's opening speech: Act 1 Scene 1 line 1 ff.

Think together to identify the contrasts Richard uses to describe the state of the country, and his own thoughts. Start by creating two drawings or colour boards to illustrate the language Richard uses:

Summer merry delightful victorious sun
Winter clouds buried bruised stern dreadful discontent

Create two cartoons of his personifications of war and peace:

grim-visaged war: weak piping time of peace / fair well-spoken days

Create a cartoon of Richard as he describes himself (don't forget to include the dogs). Annotate using Shakespeare's words.

Create Richard's Facebook page. Add a comment that uses the words he says that describe his state of mind.

Richard says he has used drunken prophecies, libel, and dreams to make his brother Edward and his brother George hate one another. He gives an example of one prophesy. Make up another perhaps more subtle prophesy that would have the same impact. Draw and annotate, or describe a dream that Edward might have had.

'Dive, thoughts, down to my soul' (line 41)

Discuss your ideas about what Richard says. How are thought and speech related? Do we think and then say what we think, or speak and then think what we say? What is the point of a soliloquy in dramatic terms, or in real life?

3 THINKING TOGETHER TIME-LINE

Shakespeare's *Richard III* and the historical Richard III – characters

Find dates of birth and death of key characters listed here.

Check dates to see how Shakespeare's story fits with what actually happened. Decide why Shakespeare alters the time-line, for example by bringing Queen Margaret into the play or by omitting the birth of Richard and Anne's son Edward of Middleham.

- Edward, George and Richard.

- Anne Neville.

- Edward of Middleham.

- Elizabeth Woodville.

- Prince Edward and Prince Richard (The Princes in the Tower).

- Queen Margaret of Anjou.

- Buckingham, Stanley, Hastings.

- Henry Richmond.

4 ACTING RICHARD III

An actor portraying Richard may have to depict all of these qualities (you can suggest others):

Malice, anger, envy, wit, hypocrisy, restlessness, courage, fiendishness, a determination to control others, dignity.

Shakespeare identified Richard as physically deformed, with a withered arm, a hunched back, and a limp. In Shakespeare's time such features were felt to reflect a person's character; we know better now.

Decide together how you would help an actor to prepare to play the part of Richard III. Can you suggest a 'role model'? Think what emphasis you would put on the lines of Richard's opening speech and his final exchange with Catesby in Scene 5. Decide if it is necessary for Richard to hobble around the stage.

Think about his costume for different scenes, deciding what effect can be achieved by what he wears. Also consider Richard's voice at different stages of the play and when he is talking to different characters – his brothers, his mother, his future wife, his allies.

Research the work of actors playing Richard III.

Consider how your group might act to depict different sides of Richard.

5 CLARENCE'S DREAM: ACT 1 SCENE 4

The poet Samuel Taylor Coleridge (1772–1834) studied Shakespeare's plays. Consider these lines from Richard III and Coleridge's *The Ancient Mariner*:

Clarence: – and often did I strive/to yield the Ghost

The Ancient Mariner: – a thousand thousand slimy things/lived on; and so did I.

Both characters, in the face of extreme suffering, will themselves to die but are unable to. Think about Clarence's dream, and the description the Ancient Mariner gives of being alone on a ship that cannot move. He is deprived of drinking water, the tropical sun stands overhead, and round his neck hangs the lucky albatross, that he shot down; all his shipmates have died.

Decide if you think Coleridge has read Clarence's dream and wants to remind us of it here.

Clarence:
O Lord, methought what pain it was to drown,
What dreadful noise of waters in my ears,
What sights of ugly death within my eyes.
Methought I saw a thousand fearful wracks,
A thousand men that fishes gnawed upon,
Wedges of gold, great anchors, heaps of pearl,
Inestimable stones, unvalued jewels,
All scattered in the bottom of the sea.
Some lay in dead men's skulls, and in the holes
Where eyes did once inhabit, there were crept –

As 'twere in scorn of eyes – reflecting gems,
That wooed the slimy bottom of the deep
And mocked the dead bones that lay scattered by

The Ancient Mariner (extracts)

The very deep did rot: O Christ!
That ever this should be!
Yea, slimy things did crawl with legs
Upon the slimy sea.

Alone, alone, all, all alone,
Alone on a wide wide sea!
And never a saint took pity on
My soul in agony.

The many men, so beautiful!
And they all dead did lie:
And a thousand thousand slimy things
Lived on; and so did I.

Beyond the shadow of the ship
I watched the water-snakes:
They moved in tracks of shining white,
And when they reared, the elfish light
Fell off in hoary flakes.

Think about Clarence's dream. Create a graphic image of what he tells us. Decide how to annotate it to show how Clarence is thinking of human life and human values; what he thinks of his own actions, and what he sees as 'fate' and inescapable.

6 RICHARD'S GHOSTS AND DREAMS: ACT 5 SCENE 3

These ghosts present themselves to Richard the night before the Battle of Bosworth Field:

- Prince Edward, son of Henry VI
- Henry VI
- George, Duke of Clarence, Richard's brother
- Earl Rivers (Anthony Woodville) brother of Queen Elizabeth
- Lord Grey, son of Queen Elizabeth

- Sir Thomas Vaughn
- Lord Hastings
- Edward V and his brother Richard, Duke of York
- Anne, Richard's wife
- Buckingham.

Create a picture or diagram of the ghosts and add speech bubbles to show what they say to Richard. Highlight all the words that are a repetition of the message of the ghosts.

Richard is now alone, and truly terrified, not of the thousands of armed men waiting to kill him, but of a sudden recognition of his own actions. Think together to follow Richard's *reasoning* in his speech as he wakes in horror, 'Give me another horse – !' *(5.3, 178–207).*

Decide if your group agrees with what he says about himself and his situation.

Discuss how Shakespeare enables us to compare Richard's attitude to himself as a 'villain' after his dream, with his way of thinking at the very start of the play.

Consider a different outcome to the battle; discuss and decide what Richard would do or say in the days and weeks ahead, if he had gained victory.

7 THINKING TOGETHER *RICHARD III*: A BAD KING OR A GOOD KING?

It remains debatable as to whether Richard had Edward and his younger brother, Richard, Duke of York, murdered in the Tower. Revisionists claim that his ally the Duke of Buckingham, or his successor, Henry Tudor had just as much cause to remove them from his path to the throne as did Richard. Opinion about his role in his nephews' disappearance has oscillated between two extremes; one is the picture painted by Shakespeare of a murderous monster who ruthlessly liquidated all who stood in his path to power, the other is of a much maligned and conscientious ruler.

(www.englishmonarchs.co.uk/plantagenet_14.htm)

Discuss these opinions; what do you think?

Thinking Together: Language use in Shakespeare's plays

Language work comes first because it gives access to everything else and it is crucial that students have confidence in using the original language of the plays as their means of access.

(Stredder 2009: 117)

. . . because Shakespeare wrote scripts, students studying his language are not confined to the question, 'What does it mean?' Other necessary questions arise from the possibilities of enactment, most obviously 'How might it be spoken and performed on stage?' Answers to such questions are never final, never definitive.

(Gibson 2005: 46)

THINKING TOGETHER: LANGUAGE USE

It is not the primary aim of this book to teach students detail of Shakespeare's complex and effective use of language; more to enable students to become involved in the life and the action of the play, and to develop their own opinions and ideas. However, the subtleties and complexities of the plays become apparent while trying to work out what is happening or while engaged with a particular scene or speech. Discussion can support learning in this area. In groups, students can collaborate to use their knowledge and reflections on the play text so that all may achieve deeper understanding. The activities included here involve, for example, considering words and phrases in some detail, using technical language, and suggesting lines and phrases from the play for analysis, evaluation and discussion.

Analysis and evaluation are higher order thinking skills. Working with a talk group can motivate students to become more involved in close study of the play texts.

The exchange of points of view can highlight what is understood – and helpfully, can lead students to confront the limit of their own knowledge or understanding. This recognition is a starting point for individual study. Discussion benefits subsequent drama or written work. Articulating ideas and listening to the ideas of others helps everyone towards a better understanding, and encourages the confidence to express opinions and reasons to a wider audience. It also informs how characters are represented in staged productions.

Students undertaking the 'language use' activities should have shared and agreed a common set of ground rules for exploratory talk, as explained in the introduction. The activities are for groups of 2–4 students, and students will need a copy of the play text.

1 SHARED THOUGHTS ABOUT WORDS

Choose one specific type of language use, e.g. *alliteration*. Think together to decide on an interesting example of this from the play. Decide what difference this use of language makes to the impact of the line, what we know about the character, or to the action of the play. Look at the Glossary for examples of language use.

Create a presentation based around your technical word.

Give the word; a definition; an example from Shakespeare's text; information about the impact of the use of language in your example; examples from other sources. Practice reading or talking through your presentation. Be prepared to explain more if asked. Each member of the group should contribute to your spoken presentation.

The whole class can take part in presentations using some of the technical vocabulary that helps us to analyse and describe Shakespeare's plays.

2 SHARED THOUGHTS ABOUT A SECTION OF THE PLAY

Select a play section of about twenty lines. Look at the Glossary for examples of language use. Check if any of the ways of using language are present in your section of the play. Identify examples of language use and say what difference the language use makes to the character, the plot, our understanding of the play, or the sound of the words.

Create a presentation based on language use in the lines you have chosen.

Give a reference for the lines; examples of language use; information about the impact of the use of language in your lines. Rehearse your presentation. Be prepared to explain more if asked. Each member of the group should contribute to this spoken presentation.

The whole class can take part in presentations to share information and understanding of some of Shakespeare's complex language use.

3 VERSE

'Verse', which originally meant simply a line, now means a group of lines (a stanza) in a poem. Blank verse is poetry that has a rhythm or meter, but does not rhyme.

Rhymed verse has rhyming end words.

The rhyme pattern can be identified by labelling the end words with letters to show which other words they rhyme with (line ending *a* rhymes with *a*, *b* with *b* and so on).

The rhymes may be couplets (aa, bb, cc) or there may be a more complicated pattern (a, b, a, b, c, c).

With your group, look at Shakespeare's text to find interesting examples of:

- blank verse (count syllables to check if the lines are iambic pentameters);

- rhyming couplets;

- another rhyme pattern.

Be prepared to share your examples and say why you think the lines are interesting and why Shakespeare uses verse in this way.

4 PROSE

Prose is ordinary speech with no pattern of rhythm or rhyme.

> Read this statement with your group:
>
> Shakespeare uses prose for everyday conversation, when there is a letter or message, when someone is mad, for comic speech or for the speech of servants.

Think together to decide if your group agrees or disagrees with this statement. What are your reasons? Find evidence in the plays to support what you think. Think how you will report back to the whole class.

5 LISTS

Shakespeare's characters use lists to build up vibrant pictures, to emphasise what they want to say, and to express strong emotions. Look at lists, for example:

- Juliet's list of all the things she would rather do than marry Paris.
- Oberon's list of flowers on the bank where Titania sleeps.
- Ophelia's list of flowers and their meanings.
- Gertrude's list of details describing Ophelia's drowning.
- Polonius' list of ways Laertes should behave in Paris.
- Egeus' list of things Lysander has done to 'bewitch' Hermia.
- Hermia's list of things she swears by when arranging to meet Lysander.
- The list of things Puck gets up to as reported by the Fairy and Puck.
- Titania's list of bad things Oberon has done.
- Titania's list of ways she and the fairies should treat Bottom.

With your group, draw and annotate a picture of the scene described.

Keep only the first item on the list. Cross out all the rest. Think together to decide the difference it would make if Shakespeare had done the same; if he had written a single item, not a list for the character to say.

Create two more items you could add to the list and discuss why they might be suitable.

6 WORD FREQUENCY COUNTS

Here are the word frequencies for '*love*' and its variations in three Shakespeare plays:

Hamlet

Love, 66; Loved, 7; Lover, 1; Loves, 7; Loving, 3.

Romeo and Juliet

Love's, 12; Love, 135; Love-devouring, 1; Love-performing, 1; Love-song, 1; Loved, 3; Lovely, 2; Lover, 4; Lovers, 8; Loves, 2; Lovest, 2; Loving, 6; Loving-jealous, 1.

Midsummer Night's Dream

Love's, 7; Love, 99; Love-in-idleness, 1; Love-juice, 2; Love-shaft, 1; Love-tokens, 1; Loved, 5; Lovely, 7; Lover's, 2; Lover, 8; Lovers, 17; Loves, 9; Lovest, 1; Loving, 1.

With your group, look at the numbers and think together to decide what this information tells us about the play.

Use the *Word Use Lists* website. Decide on a *key word* that interests you. Compare three plays by looking at the alphabetical frequencies of words in each play. Discuss whether you think that word frequency indicates anything . . . if so, what?

Key Word Examples: asleep; death; honest; life; mad; moon; tonight; wedding; word; you.

Make up a Word Use Puzzle for your class:

Choose an interesting word; find out and record its frequency in each play.

Copy your findings into a Word document and remove the title of each play.

Ask another group to predict which set of numbers belongs to which play, and why.

7 QUOTATIONS FROM THE PLAYS AS TALKING POINTS

In this activity, students work in groups to consider their own ideas about quotations from the play; the quotation is the Talking Point. Some suggested quotations for the four plays in this book are included here.

Students can be provided with questions to focus and shape their discussion if needed.

They need to know that their discussion should revolve around the ideas in the quotation; do they think the idea is right, wrong, sensible, interesting, or hard to comprehend?

The group should be prepared to share their thinking after discussion time.

Groups should offer reasons, and suggest areas of uncertainty.

Groups can usefully ask questions of their own.

Some questions to consider

- Can you say *why* what the character says is interesting, amusing or thought-provoking?

- Does it remind you of something you already knew?

- Does it teach you something?

- Can you think of reasons to agree with what the character is saying?

- Can you think of reasons to disagree?

- Can you elaborate on your own ideas, and ask others in your group for further thoughts on what they have said?

- What do you know about the character; what do you know about what is happening to them in the play? Does that influence what you think?

- Can you summarise ideas and negotiate a joint response to share with everyone?

- Can you suggest other quotations to discuss, and say why you have chosen them?

Quotations from Hamlet

Grief can be real or faked

> But I have that within which passeth show;
> These but the trappings and the suits of woe
> —*Hamlet 1.2 85–6*

Taking your own advice

> Do not, as some ungracious pastors do,
> Show me the steep and thorny way to heaven,
> Whiles, like a puff'd and reckless libertine,
> Himself the primrose path of dalliance tread
> —*Ophelia 1.3 47–50*

Listening

> Give every man thy ear, but few thy voice
> —*Polonius 1.3 68*

Lending

> Neither a borrower nor a lender be
> —*Polonius 1.3 75*

Integrity

> This above all: to thine own self be true
> —*Polonius 1.3 78*

Appearances

> That one may smile, and smile, and be a villain
> —*Hamlet 1.5 107*

Fate rules our lives

> The time is out of joint
> *Hamlet 1 5 188*

Provoking a response

> See you now;
> Your bait of falsehood takes this carp of truth
> —*Polonius 2.1 59–60*

Being concise

   – brevity is the soul of wit
                 —*Polonius 2.2 90*

Attitude

   – there is nothing either good or bad, but thinking makes it so
                 —*Hamlet 2.2 249–50*

The human race

What a piece of work is a man!
How noble in reason, how infinite in faculties,
in form and moving how express and admirable,
in action how like an angel, in apprehension how like
a god! The beauty of the world, the paragon of animals!
                 —*Hamlet 2.2 303–7*

Mercy

the less they deserve, the more merit is in your bounty
                 —*Hamlet 2.2 531–2*

Strength of character

   – blest are those
Whose blood and judgment are so well commeddled,
That they are not a pipe for Fortune's finger
To sound what stop she pleasc.
                 —*Hamlet 3.2 68–71*

Taking the long view

I must be cruel, only to be kind
                 —*Hamlet 3.4 178*

The mystery of death

Where be . . . your
flashes of merriment, that were wont to set the table on
a roar? Not one now, to mock your own grinning?
                 —*Hamlet 5.1 189–92*

Fate and free will

> Our indiscretion sometimes serves us well,
> When our deep plots do pall· and that should learn us
> There's a divinity that shapes our ends,
> Rough-hew them how we will
> —*Hamlet 5.2 8–11*

Quotations from *A Midsummer Night's Dream*

Love

> The course of true love never did run smooth
> —*Lysander 1.1 134*

Pessimism or realism

> So quick bright things come to confusion
> —*Lysander 1.1 149*

Life

> Are you sure
> That we are awake? It seems to me
> That yet we sleep, we dream.
> —*Demetrius 4.1 102*

Reticence

> Love . . . and tongue-tied simplicity
> In least speak most
> —*Theseus 5.1 104*

Agreement can include disagreement

> – never did I hear
> Such gallant chiding: for, besides the groves,
> The skies, the fountains, every region near
> Seem'd all one mutual cry: I never heard
> So musical a discord, such sweet thunder.
> *Hyppolyta 4.1 114–18*

Imagination

> Such tricks hath strong imagination,
> That if it would but apprehend some joy,
> It comprehends some bringer of that joy;
> Or in the night, imagining some fear,
> How easy is a bush supposed a bear!
> —*Theseus 5.1 18–22*

Quotations from *Romeo and Juliet*

Vulnerability

> – the weakest goes to the wall
> —*Gregory 1.1 13*

Relativity

> – one fire burns out another's burning,
> One pain is lessen'd by another's anguish
> —*Benvolio 1.2 45–6*

The provenance of dreams

> True, I talk of dreams,
> Which are the children of an idle brain,
> Begot of nothing but vain fantasy,
> Which is as thin of substance as the air
> And more inconstant than the wind
> —*Mercutio 1.4 96–100*

Experience

> He jests at scars that never felt a wound
> —*Romeo 1.2 1*

Good and evil

> Virtue itself turns vice, being misapplied;
> And vice sometimes by action dignified
> —*Friar Lawrence 2.3 21–2*

The tortoise and the hare

Too swift arrives as tardy as too slow
—Friar Lawrence 2.6 15

The power of thought

Adversity's sweet milk, philosophy,
To comfort thee
—Friar Lawrence 3.3 55–6

The meaning of life

Well we were born to die
—Capulet 3.4 4

Quotations from *Richard III*

Inhuman

Wickedness and humanity
Villain, thou know'st no law of God nor man;
No beast so fierce but knows some touch of pity.
—Lady Anne, 1.2 70

Hypocrisy

And thus I clothe my naked villany
With old odd ends stolen out of holy writ;
And seem a saint, when most I play the devil.
—Richard 1.3 343

Worst case scenario

Come, come, we fear the worst. All will be well.
—Citizen 2.3 31

Taking power – as if you didn't want it

Will you enforce me to a world of cares?
Call them again. I am not made of stone,
But penetrable to your kind entreaties
—Richard 3.7 222

The good die young

So wise so young, they say, do never live long.
—*Richard 3.1 79*

Consequences of actions

Wrong hath but wrong, and blame the due of blame.
—*Buckingham 5.1 29*

True despair

I shall despair. There is no creature loves me;
And if I die, no soul will pity me.
—*Richard 5.3 201*

The influence of hope

True hope is swift, and flies with swallow's wings;
Kings it makes gods, and meaner creatures kings.
—*Richmond 5.2 24*

8 EVERYDAY USES OF SHAKESPEARE'S WORDS

Shakespeare invented hundreds of words. Many of them are still in the common spoken and written vocabulary of English *(See References and links)*. If he needed to, he generated new words by:

- changing nouns into verbs (bet – betted)

- changing verbs into nouns (excite – excitement)

- changing verbs into adjectives (radiant – radiance; fashion – fashionable)

- adding words together (moonbeam)

- adding prefixes (vulnerable – invulnerable)

- adding suffixes (laugh – laughable)

- creating entirely new words (madcap, zany, tranquil, alligator).

Thinking Together: Using Shakespeare's words

Talk together to decide on a short contemporary scene, storyboard or song that incorporates a Shakespearean phrase. Think how to present your work so that your audience can understand the relevance of the phrase. Some phrases are suggested here – but a group or personal choice will make the work more creative.

Some phrases

- neither a borrower nor a lender be (*Hamlet*);

- brevity is the soul of wit (*Hamlet*);

- in my heart of hearts (*Hamlet*);

- what fools these mortals be (*A Midsummer Night's Dream*);

- is there no play to ease the anguish of a torturing hour (*A Midsummer Night's Dream*);

- star-crossed lovers (*Romeo and Juliet*);

- here's much to do with hate, but more with love (*Romeo and Juliet*);

- parting is such sweet sorrow (*Romeo and Juliet*).

Glossary

Alliteration: repetition of (usually) initial consonants to link words

Antithesis: to set opposites against one another – generating conflict or challenge

Assonance: repetition of vowel sounds to link words

Blank verse: unrhymed verse

Dramatic language: to evoke a scene, create mood and emotion

Iambic pentameter: a commonly used rhythm of a line. Iambic describes an unstressed syllable followed by a stressed syllable; pentameter means five of these two-syllable units in a line

Imagery: use of words to stimulate the imagination to create pictures

Irony: saying one thing but meaning another; words with meaning opposite to their literal meaning. The surface and underlying meanings of what is said are very different. Dramatic irony is when the audience knows that a character is making a mistake in what they say

Onomatopoeia: using the sound of words to convey other sounds

Oxymoron: words that are opposites linked in a phrase

Personification. turning events and circumstances into 'people' to give them life

Pun: use of different, especially ambiguous, meanings of a word for humorous effect

Repetition: repeating words or phrases to heighten their effect

Rhetoric: using persuasive language

Rhyme: matching the final sound of each line

References and links

REFERENCES

Coleridge, S.T. (1812) Essay X, *The Friend: A Series of Essays*. London: Gale & Curtis.

Dawes, L. (2012) *Talking Points: Discussion Activities in the Primary Classroom*. London: David Fulton/Routledge.

Gibson, R. (2005) *Teaching Shakespeare*. Cambridge: Cambridge University Press.

Holmes, R. (1998) *Coleridge: Darker Reflections*. London: Harper Collins/Flamingo.

Mercer, N. and Littleton, K. (2007) *Dialogue and the Development of Children's Thinking: A Sociocultural Approach*. London: Routledge.

Shakespeare, W. (1967) *A Midsummer Night's Dream*. London: Penguin Books.

Shakespeare, W. (1992) *The Tragedy of Hamlet, Prince of Denmark*. Hertfordshire: Wordsworth Classics.

Shakespeare, W. (1968) *King Richard The Third*. Harmondsworth: Penguin Books.

Shakespeare, W. (1937) *Romeo and Juliet*. London: Penguin Books.

Stredder, J. (2009) *The North Face of Shakespeare: Activities for Teaching the Plays*. Cambridge: Cambridge University Press.

FURTHER READING

Greenblatt, S., Cohen, W., Howard, J F, and Eisaman Maus, K. (eds) (1997) *The Norton Shakespeare*. Oxford: Norton.

Malless, S., McQuain, J. and Blechman, R.O. (1998) *Coined by Shakespeare: Words and Meanings First Penned by the Bard*. Springfield, MA: Merriam-Webster.

Sher, A. (1986) *The Year of the King: An Actor's Diary*. London: Nick Hern Books. (A diary about preparation for the role of Richard III at Stratford upon Avon in 1985.)

WEB LINKS

Blank verse in Shakespeare

www.shakespeare-online.com/plays/romeoandjuliet/romeohudsonverse.html

Blank verse and rhyme in *Romeo and Juliet*

www.shakespeare-online.com/plays/romeoandjuliet/romeohudsonverse.html

Blogging Shakespeare – some links

www.60-minutes.bloggingshakespeare.com

Bosworth battlefield

www.bosworthbattlefield.com

Coleridge on *Romeo and Juliet*

http://absoluteshakespeare.com/guides/romeo_and_juliet/characters/romeo_and_juliet_characters_essay.htm

Coleridge on *Hamlet*

http://absoluteshakespeare.com/guides/hamlet/essay/hamlet_essay.htm

Clinical depression – information adapted from

www.mayoclinic.com/health/depression/DS00175/DSECTION=symptoms

***Hamlet* – David Tennant**

www.bbc.co.uk/programmes/b00pk71s

Monologues

www.shakespeare-monologues.org

No fear Shakespeare

http://nfs.sparknotes.com

Richard III

www.englishmonarchs.co.uk/plantagenet_14.htm

Romeo and Juliet – full play script

www.william-shakespeare.info/script-text-romeo-and-juliet.htm

Romeo and Juliet: What's going on?

www.beyondbooks.com/sha91/5.asp

Shakespeare online

www.shakespeare-online.com

Shakespeare quotations

http://shakespeare-navigators.com/dream/quotesdream.html

Soliloquies

https://sites.google.com/a/shakespearereadsfreud.com/www/Home/solid-flesh-or-sullied—1

Tibert the cat in the Reynard stories

www.freefictionbooks.org/books/c/2832-the-comical-creatures-from-wurtemberg-by-unknown?start=13

Themes in *Romeo and Juliet*

www.shakespeare-online.com/playanalysis/romeocommentary.html

Thinking Together Information and resources for teachers

thinkingtogether.educ.cam.ac.uk

T.S. Eliot on *Hamlet*

www.bartleby.com/200/sw9.html
www.gradesaver.com/midsummer-nights-dream

Vygotsky's essay on *Hamlet*

www.marxists.org/archive/vygotsky/works/1925/art8.htm

Walpole's historic doubts – *Richard III*

www.r3.org/bookcase/walpole/walpole4.html

Wattpad: Holden Caulfield on *Romeo and Juliet*

www.wattpad.com/312286-cather-and-the-rye?p=45

Words Shakespeare invented

http://shakespeare-online.com/biography/wordsinvented.html
www.nosweatshakespeare.com/resources/shakespeare-words

Youtube – Blackadder helps Bill edit 'To be or not to be'

www.youtube.com/watch?v=3jc-7cT12gE&feature=relate